THE GILLETTE BOOK OF
CRICKET AND FOOTBALL

The Gillette Book

of

Cricket and Football

Edited by
GORDON ROSS

THE GILLETTE SAFETY RAZOR COMPANY

CONTENTS

ILLUSTRATIONS

THE CHALLENGE

When I was invited by Gillette to produce a book on cricket and football with the principal aim of helping young players, I saw it not only as an intriguing prospect, but also as a challenge, for it is the fostering and stimulating of the young player of today which ultimately produces the great player of tomorrow. It may be, for example, that in a few years time a great player, looking nostalgically back through a distinguished career, will remember a piece of advice which has stood him in good stead, and which he found within the pages of this book. If that happens even once, then this book has fulfilled the purpose I had in mind.

Sport today has become Universal and many countries have come a long way in a very short time by using new methods and varying techniques. This book, therefore, could only be contemporary by covering the broadest possible front. In the pages that follow, great players of the world give their views – a West Indian, a South African, an Argentinian, a Hungarian, yet all names known from one corner of the world to the other. How does a young West Indian become one of cricket's finest all-rounders, or a young Argentinian, who began by kicking orange peel, develop into the highest paid footballer in the world? Sobers and di Stefano tell their own story, as a shining example to be followed.

Gillette, whose interest in sport is well enough known, have chosen an eminently worthwhile subject. I only hope that the finished product will, in some way or another, achieve its aim in lending valuable assistance to the young players of our two national games.

GORDON ROSS,
Editor.

THE MANY FACETS OF CRICKET

Of the many facets of cricket which are the concern of M.C.C. one of the most important is undoubtedly the coaching of young players. The game can only thrive if the future generation have an interest in and a desire to play it, and it is M.C.C.'s duty to see that it does.

The M.C.C. Youth Cricket Association was originally formed with the object of interesting the Youth of the country in this great game, and I am delighted that its Chairman, Mr. H. S. Altham, has written so splendidly in this book underlining the value of coaching. It gave me, too, a very great deal of pleasure to learn of Gillette's interest in the welfare of the game and that coaching was to be the main theme of this book. There could have been no better choice of subject, nor, indeed, could Gillette have chosen an editor for the book who has the game closer to his heart than Mr. Gordon Ross, who as an author of cricket books and a writer on the game is so well known to us at Lord's.

The M.C.C. Committee's decision to be associated with this book was entirely spontaneous, and we are most grateful to Gillette for their efforts in spreading the gospel of cricket in such a thoroughly commendable way. I wish the book and everyone who reads it all possible success.

S. C. GRIFFITH,
Secretary, M.C.C.

THE RAPID GROWTH OF FOOTBALL

The Football Association is exceedingly proud of being the oldest parent association of football, a game which has rapidly grown in world popularity as is shown by the fact that more than one hundred national associations are now affiliated to the World Organization of F.I.F.A.

Many of these countries have used the services of players and coaches from England to help in the development of the game. Indeed, we are all aware of the importance of drawing upon the experience of top players and coaches in our efforts to improve playing standards.

I am sure that this book will be widely read and, in consequence, it will play a useful part in stimulating players to give thought to new ideas to improve their play.

DENIS FOLLOWS,
Secretary,
The Football Association.

CRICKET

THE CONTRIBUTORS –

> H. S. Altham
>
> Colin Cowdrey
>
> Neil Adcock
>
> David Allen
>
> Arthur McIntyre
>
> Garfield Sobers
>
> Trevor Bailey
>
> Frank Lee
>
> Gordon Ross

The Value of Coaching

By Harry Altham
(Chairman, M.C.C. Youth Cricket Association)

THERE would appear to be a tendency in some quarters today to question, even to discredit, the value of coaching in cricket. The critics – and some of them past players of distinction – denounce it as fatally cramping to the young player's natural gifts, forcing him into a uniform and disastrously limited mould which robs his playing of the colour, zest, and variety which it would otherwise command, and by so doing accounts in large measure for the problems with which first-class cricket is today admittedly faced.

It is because, after fifty years of trying to help boy cricketers, I am utterly convinced that this is not true, that I welcome so warmly the enterprise of Messrs. Gillette in producing this book on coaching, and appreciate their asking me to try to write something in it.

There have always been Jeremiahs about cricket: even before the last century ended, and again during what is sometimes still referred to as the "Golden Age" of the early 1900s, some eminent old players were saying that the game was not what it was, or what it should be, though none of them, so far as I know, then laid the blame at the coach's door.

Of course first-class cricket today has difficulties to face: there is the ever-mounting spiral of its costs, the ever-increasing competition for its potential supporters from other forms of relaxation and enjoyment, and the much greater mobility which so many of them can command: full employment, too, must surely be a factor. But how wrong should we be to think of cricket primarily in terms of the first-class game: the cricket that really matters, and will always matter most, is not that played at Lord's or the Oval, Old Trafford or Melbourne, under the shadow of Table Mountain or beside the Caribbean Sea. It is the cricket played on its native home of the village green, on the private grounds of countless Clubs, in the public Parks, even in the dark streets or waste ground of our industrial towns, with a lamp post or a pile of coats for a wicket, and every boy a Statham or a Trueman, a Cowdrey, May, or Dexter in his heart.

On that yardstick I have no fear for this game which Englishmen evolved, no one knows how many centuries ago, and which they have since then taught the world – or so much of it – to play and love as they do themselves. Never, I am convinced, have more boys been playing it than today, and playing it better, and so getting from it all that cricket can give, and never have they been helped by more, and more skilful and more devoted, coaches.

LOOK, LISTEN, AND LEARN

"But," I can hear the critics say, "that is just the assumption that on this wider front we still challenge: Does all this coaching in fact help them? Would not they be better off if left to work out their own salvation, and to follow their natural instincts for hitting and bowling, stopping, catching, and throwing a ball?" My immediate answer is that surely they are arguing against the known facts as revealed in the whole general field of athletic skills. The marvellous technique of the Brazil footballers was not the result of some "natural evolution", but the climax of a long and arduous preparation in which from boyhood they were helped and trained first to understand the complex problems of ball control and positioning, and then to practise and to master them. The supreme ability of a Rod Laver or an Arnold Palmer are of course rooted in natural gifts of eye and sinew, balance and timing, but they could never have reached the peaks they have attained if they had not been ready, from the time they started to play, to look and to listen and to learn. Is not this true, too, for what is surely the much simpler problem of moving two legs round a running track? Would not Herbert Elliot and Peter Snell be the first to admit their debt to those who coached them? And how, then, do the critics of coaching fare when we come to the field of cricket? The whole of cricket history challenges them. Was not William Beldham, greatest of all batsmen in the Hambledon era, coached by Harry Hall, the gingerbread maker of Farnham? Did not W. G. always look back with gratitude to the coaching he had when a small boy in the family orchard net from his uncle Pocock, and to his formidable mother's insistence that if he concentrated on playing straight, he would go one better than even his greatly gifted, but unorthodox, elder brother E. M.? Were not the very foundations of Australian cricket laid by Lawrence and Caffyn, who stayed behind to coach in that country after our first two tours there? And, to come down to today, would not Sir Leonard Hutton agree that the foundations of his batting were laid in the Headingley nets, and Messrs. May, Cowdrey, Dexter, and Sheppard say the same about the coaching they had at their schools? "Ah," comes the quick rejoinder, "what about the greatest of them all, Sir Donald Bradman? He was never coached, and look at what he was and did." The answer to that, I think, is that Sir Donald was a phenomenon from which it is dangerous to argue. First, he had extraordinary gifts of eye, speed of reaction, and physical co-ordination; second, he had, and I may add has, an exceptionally astute analytical mind, coupled with icy concentration and relentless determination. What he did in fact was to coach himself by watching, analysing, and then by unremitting practice, even by himself, working out what he wanted to be able to do with a bat, exactly how it should be done, and then getting down to doing it until he was satisfied – and Sir Donald is not easily content. Surely, too, it is significant that he, the outstanding "natural" batsman of his own, or perhaps any, generation, should also be the author of one of the best coaching books ever produced. Clearly Sir Donald believes that there is a technique in cricket which in fact pays, and one that can be both taught and learnt.

BASIC BACKGROUND

Nor is it surprising when we look a bit closer at the problem. The basic background is the plain fact that cricket is not a natural game: we walk, we run, we write, we drive, we ride "full chested", but cricket whether batting, bowling, or fielding (except in pure defence) must be played sideways. If we pick up a club or a bat – the words are in fact synonymous – our natural instinct is to grip it more tightly with the bottom hand and to swing it crosswise: but that is exactly what you must not do at the crease if you want to stay there: you have got to hold on with the top hand, and swing it not across but down the line of the ball. To play a forward or back stroke right means mastering what is very far from being a natural movement, but master it you can, if you are shown how, and master it you must, if you are to be able to stay at the wicket long enough to exploit whatever natural ability you have for hitting the ball. And when it comes to attack, what a reinforcement to that natural ability it is when the coach explains that the wider the off half-volley you want to drive, the more you must turn the back of the left shoulder on the bowler and lead with it out and on to the line: that the secret of all on-driving lies in the initial dip of the left shoulder, and that if you want to cut securely and effectively, you just must pick your bat up high, and that you cannot do that if your right elbow is tucked into your side. Even in the "natural" cross bat strokes the young player will not unaided realize that if he is to play them safely and effectively he has got to get his head on to the line of the ball, and then keep it still, and that the ball should be hit with a whip of the arms and hands, and not by any heave of the body.

It is just the same with bowling and fielding. However naturally gifted a boy may be, he can only make the most of those gifts by being helped to understand the right techniques, and encouraged to persevere in practising and mastering them. To take two simple examples – how many young bowlers realize unaided the importance of keeping their left shoulder pointed at the target as long as possible in the act of delivery? And how many young fielders automatically "get down early", stay down, and watch the ball right into their hands?

"THE WORST OF SINS"

I could continue on these lines almost indefinitely; suffice it to say that in every department of the game there are basic principles which all the great players have in fact observed far more than they have ever disregarded. But to coach boys in them should never mean that we turn out "robots" playing on a uniform pattern. The end product will inevitably vary within wide limits according to a boy's "make up", whether of physique, temperament, or that indefinable something which we call "ball sense": the worst of all coaching sins is to stop a boy from hitting, still more from wanting to hit, the ball. But the more he can be helped to hit it right, the better chance he will have of going on hitting it.

Then, of course, there is the wider and fascinating field of the mental approach to the game, and of "cricket tactics". Playing an innings means more than just playing a sequence of strokes: it means pitting your wits and your will against an ever-varying set of problems whether in terms of the bowlers, the pitch, the clock, or even your partner at the other end. A bowler, too, will find one batsman, or one state of the wicket, setting him a totally different problem from another: a placing of the field that makes sense against "X" or at 2.15, may make nonsense against "Y" or at 3.45. Above all, a cricket captain is faced with a ceaseless and complex challenge by this game of sudden vicissitudes, and ever and subtly changing balance. In all this field there can be no substitute for experience, and it is to the coach's greater experience and riper judgement that the boy must look.

Finally, let me try to say a word or two about something equally important as, perhaps more important than, any issue of technique or tactics – I mean the personal relationship between the young cricketer and his coach. The coaching of cricket is an exacting, an exhausting, even at times a frustrating, job. To coach a keen and gifted young player should be sheer delight, but not all are gifted, and not all are always as keen as a coach could wish. Here is the real challenge, to infuse such a boy with his own enthusiasm, and to help him make the very best of such ability as he may have. And the secret of it? That he should care about each boy he coaches, and make him feel that he cares: that he should never be content with second best whether in his own effort or in his pupil's, above all that he should encourage and inspire.

KEEP TRYING

But of course this is a two-way traffic: no matter how competent and keen the coach is, it is the young cricketer himself, and the effort that he is prepared to make, which must have the last word. May I then, now nearing the end of a pretty long, but wonderfully happy, cricket road, say just this to him? Cricket is a hard taskmaster, and there is no easy way to success: it demands all you can give to her in body and mind and will. There are times when the sun will shine and all will go well with you: enjoy them, and be thankful for them, but never be satisfied: success should never be a peak, but only and always a spur from which you aim at something higher. There are times, too – don't we all know them? – when nothing will go right, when you are out of form and feel you will never regain it, or, more trying still, when you know you are batting or bowling well and yet fortune, that fickle goddess, turns her head aside and the runs and wickets just will not come. Then you must harden your heart, and keep trying, and in the end she will smile again. Never forget that you are one of a team, and that the spirit and enjoyment of a team depends on the attitude and the effort of each player in it. Others beside yourself may be finding the game a struggle: your stout heart and cheerful face may help them, too, to fight their way through.

And the reward of it all? Of that we may be certain: the joy of health and strength harnessed to an art and to a venture, the friends that it brings to us, even if on the field they are foes, and when you take off your pads, whether for the day, for the season, or after long years for good, the memory of troubles halved and joys doubled, because both have been shared with them.

Colin Cowdrey,

one of the world's greatest batsmen talks about his craft

When he was injured against West Indies Colin Cowdrey had already played in 64 Test matches for England and in 1957 against West Indies at Birmingham he participated in a fourth wicket stand of 411 with Peter May. A magnificent all-round games player – rackets, tennis, squash, golf, Cowdrey's highest score is 307 for M.C.C. against South Australia last winter. Cowdrey was once aptly described as a batsman out of the top drawer.

As you prepare to hit the perfect golf shot the problem, considerable as it is, can be easily understood. There are only two issues at stake.

First, one has to decide upon the best line to the hole and this involves being able to judge distance after making the right allowances for wind. After that it is purely a question of swinging the club correctly. Every golf stroke requires the same perfectly grooved swing.

It is a very difficult game to master I am sure, but I wish the art of batsmanship was as straightforward in principle. The good batsman has to become proficient in a host of different skills.

He has to be able to hit the ball on the off-side with left shoulder leading and the top hand doing most of the work. If the bowler alters his line of attack to the leg-stump, he then has to give himself enough room to hit the ball wide of mid-on or off his legs through mid-wicket.

He has got to learn to play the swinging ball when it is new and the wicket fresh. He has to learn to play the spinning ball not only when the wicket is wet and the ball is taking out pieces and lifting, but also on the dry, dusty wicket which begins to crumble on the third day.

A SHREWD EYE

He has got to learn to watch the bowler's hand and detect his variations and tricks. He has to learn to concentrate . . . and keep concentrating. He has got to acquire a shrewd eye with regard to the field positions set against him, calculating their tactics and pre-selecting gaps for the loose delivery.

Above all, he must have courage; courage in abundance. Batting in a crisis requires mental courage which will accept the circumstances with an equable calm and play each ball on its merits regardless of a tense atmosphere and crouching fielders breathing down the neck. Batting against fast bowling demands the physical courage which will not flinch at anything. There are so many sides to the art of batting that it is hard to know where to begin a coaching brief.

With the seven-year-old youngster it must be right for his coach to let him have his head and thereby acquire the "feel" of hitting the ball hard and high. "Cow-shots" are quite permissible. The important thing is that he is learning to use his eye, wrists, and power – the essential ingredients which go to make up this mysterious gift of timing. A sense of timing is usually in-born in the natural games players, but it still has to be brought out. Too much coaching at an early age with the accent on correctness can stifle the natural freedom of stroke.

"COW-SHOT CORNER"

There comes a time with the promising youngster when the coach will intervene occasionally pleading for a straighter bat to the awkward length ball, whilst insisting that the full toss or long hop should be despatched with gay exhilaration. The difficult problem which besets the youngster is this question of length, for he has to learn why one delivery requires a forward stroke and another a back stroke. Every ball to his eye deserves the same fate – the full-blooded swing to "Cow-shot Corner". It is the gentle persuasion on the part of the mentor which can instruct the youngster in the arts of discretion at the same time not discouraging him from hitting the ball hard.

I am sure that it is important that the young cricketer is encouraged to keep hitting the ball hard. It is a habit which comes easily to the youngster whereas the adult finds it difficult to adapt his game. In any case, it is the sheer thrill of lashing a half-volley through the covers which provides the stimulus required to make the young player strive harder to reach the top. Without this exciting experience, the game would be very drab indeed. There comes a time in his natural development when he learns to apply the perfectly played stroke to the right ball, and herein lies his graduation to maturity. It is one thing to be able to play the stroke correctly and it is quite essential to learn to wait for the right moment to play it. This can only come through trial and error of experience.

Having got to the stage where the batsman can play all the strokes and can choose the right ball for each stroke, only one problem remains – can he stay at the wicket long enough to be able to produce his array of strokes? The key to all batting then, lies in a sound defence. So then, just as with a well-balanced innings, let us begin with a period of defence and play ourselves in.

THE STANCE

Although I like a stance with feet nine inches apart, left shoulder leading and hiding the right shoulder from the bowler, each batsman must be allowed his own little mannerisms. He must feel comfortable and able to move his feet very quickly. He must have a good vision of the ball with the face fully turned to the bowler and both eyes level with the ground. Basically, all defence can be reduced to a quick movement of the feet forward or back, and a very strong top hand. A quick movement of the feet because you are only going to defend against the good length ball, and either the front foot is thrust out to the pitch of the ball to scotch spin, swing, or lift, or the back foot is pushed back towards the wicket to give you as much time as possible to see any irregularity off the pitch. In either case the head moves onto the line of the ball thus ensuring that the bat will be in the perpendicular position.

Now, the top hand takes over steering the bat down the line of the ball down out of harm's way. The fingers of the right hand do no more than help to guide the bat along the line and supporting the demands of the left hand.

So, to the good length, or half-volley side of good length ball, push the front foot to as near the pitch of the ball, with head in line, eye glued to the ball; let the left hand lead the bat through and at the moment of impact you should find the chin, the left wrist, and left toe in perpendicular line. Practise this movement in front of a mirror until you feel it comes naturally. You will find this the most important part of your game.

The same applies to the back stroke. To anything short of a good length, back and over onto the line, head in line, eye glued to the pitch of the ball with a conscious tight grip of the top hand as it leads the full face of the bat through to meet it.

THE GAPS

As you gain in confidence with these strokes, you will find yourself having sufficient time occasionally to see the ball off the wicket and steer it with the left hand into a gap in the field for a short single. Hence you are turning strict defence into offence very cleverly; this is often the safest way of starting an innings.

During my Test innings of 182 at the Oval against Pakistan David Sheppard and I could only muster 76 before lunch. This was against some very accurate bowling. Finding few loose balls to hit I had to resort to the quick single and of the 90 balls I received before lunch, 24 of my 32 runs were placed singles. This felt very hard work at the time but it proved to be the basis of a large innings.

Every innings needs building in stages. True, that in one-day cricket there is not the time to squander two hours over 32 runs but every player needs three full overs acclimatizing himself to the conditions before he allows himself the liberty of opening his shoulders. This is the time to look for ten singles in those first eighteen balls and if you are successful you have given yourself an encouraging start to the innings.

Now look for the gaps in the field. Nearly every over will bring one loose ball, and it is good batting to know, before it is bowled, where you can best hit it. BUT beware of one simple and fatal fault. When you are over-anxious to hit the ball through a particular gap, you tend to lift the head and look towards it before the ball is struck. Have the gap in your "mind's eye" but keep your real eyes on the ball. Placing the ball for the single and pre-selecting the gap for the powerful stroke make up the ingredients for a good innings. Remember, a stroke beautifully executed which sends the ball straight to a fielder with no run scored is of very little help to anybody . . . except the fieldsman!

Neil Adcock,

Great South African Test Player,
discusses fast bowling

This fine South African fast-bowler with the smooth-flowing action has represented his country in 24 Tests and has taken 95 wickets. One of the most popular players ever to come to England he made full use of his height – 6 feet, 3 inches, and took 6 for 43 in an innings against Australia.

FAST bowlers who shatter the wickets with sheer speed and batsmen who effortlessly crack sixes into the stands will always thrill the spectators and especially young schoolboys. As I cannot reveal the formula for "six hitting" I shall however endeavour to pass on a few hints on fast bowling which I hope will prove helpful to any budding "quickies".

Whenever a new fast bowler is chosen for his county, province or country, the first thing everyone, including the opposition wants to know is, "Is he as fast as Larwood? Does he move the ball? Can he bowl for long periods? Is he accurate? Can he bowl an effective bouncer? Can he bowl on all types of wickets?" If the answer was "yes" to every one of those questions, then indeed a super bowler would have been unearthed.

In case we think that no fast bowler can produce all these attributes, cast your minds back to some of the post-war fast bowlers seen in Test cricket. Lindwall, Miller, Statham, and Trueman have all mastered the arts of fast bowling and at the height of their careers could make the ball move or pitch in the manner in which they intended.

These same bowlers did not become a force in international cricket overnight. Days and weeks of hard training, net practice, assiduous devotion to their task when bowling and listening and learning as much about the game as possible, earned these bowlers the highest honours the game can offer.

Many promising young pace bowlers have come to me to assist them in improving their pace, direction, or movement. Remember that not all of these things can be done at once. Each must be tackled in turn and slowly perfected until you feel that you have complete control of the ball.

The most important factor is length and direction. You may be the fastest bowler in your club but you would never be any good to your side by hurling down the ball well outside the off and leg stump. Make the batsman play at every delivery if possible. Try to concentrate on a target, no matter how small, and from twenty-two yards with a stubborn batsman in front of them, the wickets sometimes do look very small indeed. Make the off-stump, which in most cases can be seen, your target, and bowl the ball to pitch on a spot which would have the batsman stretching forward to cover the delivery. If practising in the nets without a batsman it is always a good idea to place a sheet of newspaper on a spot covering the perfect length and endeavour to pitch on this spot. Many famous bowlers have gained their accuracy in this manner.

A GIFT

Let us move on to the next phase – pace and how to increase it. Remember that genuine pace is as much a gift as classic batsmanship is and therefore not all aspiring quick bowlers can produce that extra yard of pace that will lift them out of the fast-medium into the express class. A fast bowler when operating, and I generalize in this case, is like a car engine. To be in perfect running order everything must move smoothly and rhythmically for after running eighteen or twenty paces, then propelling a ball the length of the wicket at speeds reaching 85 m.p.h. there is very little margin for error. The run-up to the wicket should not be too long as this will tire you unnecessarily. There is no golden rule as to how many paces you should run, but mainly that you should have a run that is comfortable. This can only be achieved by trial and error at the nets. Don't sprint the length of your run, rather start with a slow trot gradually increasing in pace until by the time you have reached the bowling crease you are perfectly balanced to use your body plus the speed of your run to let the ball go at its fastest. A bowler who sprints to the wicket then checks himself before delivering the ball, might just as well run off three paces. It is the smoothness of your run plus the rhythmic movement of the body and arms in the delivery stride, that will assist you in achieving the pace you desire.

Speed is the fast bowler's main attacking weapon but don't be misled into thinking that speed alone will bring the satisfaction of seeing wickets tumble. An opening batsman's job apart from keeping his wicket intact, is to see the shine off the new ball. Once he has done this he will have gauged the speed of the wicket and will then start using *your* speed off the wicket to drive you through the covers. It is a well-known fact that a ball driven from a fast bowler travels quicker through the covers than off a slow bowler. What is the answer to this? Being able to move a cricket ball either in the air or off the wicket will induce a batsman into playing across the line of flight and perhaps causing his dismissal. A word of warning on this point. Don't try to bowl too many different deliveries. Rather concentrate on bowling a stock ball such as the inswinger, and occasionally, perhaps no more than once an over, varying it by bowling an away swinger or leg-cutter.

VICIOUS INSWINGER

Let me quote you a story of my own case. For years all I could bowl apart from sheer speed was a vicious inswinger. Although this was successful, the leading batsmen I opposed soon knew that every delivery would swing into them and before long they had countered it, and were scoring freely on the leg-side. It was then that I decided to try and perfect the outswinger. I bought a book written by that excellent pre-war England bowler Bill Bowes and practised for many a day at the nets. When I first put my new-found weapon into practice I was hit all over the field, but slowly I mastered it. In the last few years of my career I still bowled the inswinger, but kept the outswinger which by now was a fast leg-cutter as an extra variety and in most cases it produced the result I wanted.

I wonder how many bowlers in all classes of cricket ever stop to think about scheming a batsman out. Many a boy is content to fling down the ball all day in the hope that the batsman will make a mistake and cause his dismissal. Before that careless stroke comes along he may have already compiled a tidy score and your bowling analysis will have suffered somewhat. Watch the batsman's footwork and see if he is essentially a forward or back foot player. Here your length must be altered accordingly. Does he have a high back lift and if so an occasional yorker will have a good chance of getting through. Some players do not counter the short pitched bouncer at all well and an occasional delivery such as this directed on a line of the middle and off stump is a particularly awkward one to play. Here again I must emphasize that it is not overdone as the surprise value of the bouncer will be overcome by its frequency.

Field placing for your bowling is normally handled by your captain, but you must assist him by suggesting your ideas and bowling to your field. At the start of a game and with the new ball in use the normal field placings are three slips, gully, two leg-slips, short square leg (in front of square), mid-off, and mid-on. This field gives you eight men in close catching positions, but remember that your covers have only one man guarding them. On green fast wickets and under conditions suitable for moving the ball, this field can be employed whenever the fast bowler is operating.

When the ball has lost its shine or the wicket has become easy paced, then move your third slip to cover, a leg-slip to fine-leg and short square-leg to mid-wicket. This will still allow you to have men in close catching positions behind the wicket in addition to covering the gaps in front of the wicket.

Fast bowling is physically the most strenuous part of cricket and to give of your best let alone enjoy it, you must be perfectly fit. The shoulders, body, and legs come under a terrific pounding when bowling for long periods and it is understandable that the pace men suffer more injuries than any other players. Strengthen your legs by running round and round a field interspersed with short sprints. For the shoulders and back, a series of press-ups and toe-touching is recommended. Lying on your back and raising and lowering the legs will harden the stomach muscles, which must be strong when using the body in the delivery stride. A final piece of advice before going on to bowl. Always warm up beforehand by swinging the arms and bending the knees, as this is the time when you are most likely to pull any muscles. Ray Lindwall used to loosen up thoroughly in the dressing room before going out to bowl, so that he could deliver the first ball at top pace and on the wicket. By this he was nearly always able to achieve an early break through.

The Fascination of Spin Bowling

By David Allen

David Allen has had the difficult role in England's side of
following Jim Laker as the off-spinner. He has now played
in nineteen Tests and has shown his qualities as a batsman as
well as a bowler. In 1961 he scored 121 not out for Gloucestershire against Notts at Trent Bridge; a year earlier in Bradford
he had taken 8 wickets for 41 against Yorkshire.

THERE is no other skill in our game of cricket that takes
so many years to master as slow bowling. People have often
asked me why this should be, because after all, one only has
to learn the basic principles of this art as do batsmen and
fast bowlers in theirs, but is this really true? Is there so much
to be learned after one has control of length, direction, and
spin?

One of the most important pieces of a slow bowler's
equipment is his flight. To give the batsman the wrong
impression of where a ball is pitching or to make him misjudge the speed is one of the chief weapons of a bowler,
especially when the wicket is good and is not responsive to spin.

Test match wickets nowadays are made to last five days
in our country and often six days abroad; this has meant
that groundsmen have leant towards batsmen a great deal
and the majority of Test wickets are good.

INTERESTING SUBJECTS

Wickets are an interesting subject from a spinner's point of
view in that he has to be able to size up a pitch as quickly as
possible to know how he will bowl on it and what kind of
field setting he will have for himself.

Abroad, pitches tend to be very good with much less grass
on them than there is in England, but the spinner will often
find that the pace or bounce of the pitch will give him a
certain amount of help. A great many people do not realize
that the worst wicket to bowl on is a very good English
wicket where the pace and bounce of the ball off the wicket
is less than abroad, thus easing the task of the batsmen.

The easy pace of our wickets in these modern days has
cut down the use of the leg-spinner, who likes the wickets
with pace and bounce in them. Although one can afford not

to have a leg-spinner in the side in England he is worth his weight in gold on wickets abroad; this can easily be proved by looking at Richie Benaud's performances in Australia and in addition in India and Pakistan.

Quite often abroad although one finds beautiful wickets the same thing cannot be said for their outfields which are found to be rough with little growth of grass once again. This also can be to the spinner's advantage in that unlike England, where the shine may stay on the ball a long time, the ball may be very rough after only a dozen overs and much easier to grip.

Having spoken generally about wickets and conditions that spinners meet at home and abroad I would like to progress to consider the way one has to bowl on these wickets to these batsmen.

The overseas cricketer coming from wickets that are generally good for stroke making is obviously a different proposition from the English batsman where the ball is often on top of the bat.

FIRST OBSERVATION

The first observation that one makes is that they are not afraid of getting away from the line of the ball when playing a shot, their reactions through playing on faster wickets than us are quicker and this makes them good "square cutters" and adept at moving down to the wicket to drive the ball.

How does the spinner combat this kind of attack on him by the batsmen on very good wickets? One of the main rules for the natural spinner to remember is that he must always keep his direction, once he fails in that the batsmen get on top. There is a great saying abroad amongst bowlers when they are on such good pitches, "I will bowl straight – and if they miss I hit". I always bowl at the off-stump myself knowing that any time the batsman takes a liberty I have a good chance of bowling him out as well as of getting him out in many other ways.

It is also the bowler's job to study his batsman; he may be a person that likes to get his runs quickly and plays a desperation shot when he is tied down for three or four overs; he might play more on one side of the wicket than the other or he could be a bad starter of an innings. Although these may only be small points, on good wickets they are all worth considering.

Natural spinners abroad are not used as the main attacking force, this is left to the fast bowlers and the leg-spin and googly bowler. The leg-spinner's skill is a difficult one to master, so much depends on temperament because from day to day one can never expect to know what kind of form he is in, it is the leg-spinner's temperament to be able to come back after he has taken a lot of stick that makes him a good bowler. On good wickets the leg-spinner has always got a chance of turning the ball and with a natural flight that comes with this, they are always difficult bowlers to play when dropping the ball on a length.

ALL DIFFERENT

The leg-spinner also has the trick of bowling the googly and the top spinner, all with the same action. A man who has made a study of this department of the game is the Australian captain, Richie Benaud, and I remember batting against him in 1961 and he bowled me five different balls in one over and to all intents and purposes all with the same action. Richie also always kept plugging away at the batsmen, even on good wickets, consistently dropping on a good length on the middle and off stump.

Jim Laker and Hughie Tayfield were natural spinners, who towards the end of their careers must have learnt as much as anyone has ever known about spin bowling.

Laker was the genuine finger spinner who "tweaked" the ball a great deal, towards the end of his career he was one of the most knowledgeable spinners I have ever met, he could sum up a cricket situation from a slow bowler's point of view so easily. At his peak he was the ideal slow bowler able to bowl on every type of wicket.

The same could not be said for Hughie Tayfield who was really a better bowler on a good wicket than a bad one and that is where he earned his reputation, he directed his off-spinners at the middle and off stump but he had a natural tendency to swing the ball away towards first slip which gave him an added weapon on good wickets, apart from his natural flighting of the ball.

Sonny Ramadhin was another of the great slow bowlers I have played against and watched with great interest, his asset was that he developed something that was different, that not many people had seen before; he bowled the ball turning both ways as does the leg-break and googly bowler yet always delivered the ball from the front of his hand.

33

An interesting point was that although English batsmen had difficulty in playing Ramadhin throughout his first English tour they all played him much easier abroad, not only were the wickets better but the atmosphere and light were so good that one could pick his leg-spinner in the air and play him off the wicket.

Having named some of the best spin bowlers I have had the pleasure of playing against one turns one's thoughts to the batsmen who are good players of spin bowling.

One that instantly springs to one's mind is Neil Harvey, who is a great stroke player and never appears to misjudge the length of a ball even when going down the wicket to a bowler.

Garfield Sobers is an elegant player who hits the bad ball as hard as anyone. Of our own batsmen I am sure that none has a better technique than Colin Cowdrey and even on a wicket that really helps the bowler his bat still appears to be as wide as a barn door.

As a final thought on spin bowling I always remember the words of the experienced England captain who said to me before my first Test match "Do the simple things well" – I am sure he is right.

Arthur McIntyre, Surrey and England
now the Surrey coach, talks about wicket-keeping

Arthur McIntyre – "Mac" – was the wicket-keeper for Surrey
during their golden years of seven successive Championships.
He played three times for England and when he retired in
1958 many admirers thought this was far too soon. He did so,
however, to fill the vacant post of Coach to Surrey, a job he
is now doing with distinction. Scored 143 against Kent at
Blackheath in 1949.

IT is not possible to have kept wicket in first-class cricket
for as long as I did without forming hard and fast opinions
on how young wicket-keepers should be coached. This does
not mean that I have revolutionary ideas on the game, in
fact I believe that quite the best book for any youngster who
has ambitions to make himself into a good cricketer is the
M.C.C. Cricket Coaching book which is full of invaluable
information compiled after a good deal of thought by people
who not only have the game at heart but have the knowledge as well. This is very important, and is why I firmly
believe that a wicket-keeper can only be coached by a
wicket-keeper. It is too much a specialist position for, say, a
seam bowler or an opening batsman to turn his hand to
coaching wicket-keepers. The wicket-keeper, if only because
of the law of averages, is the key man in the field. He gets
more opportunities to win or to lose matches than any of his
colleagues; after all, only a small percentage of a bowler's
wickets are clean bowled, and on a wicket where the ball is
either turning for the spinners or moving about for the seam
bowlers the most likely way of getting wickets is by the batsman playing and just getting a touch, so that the wicket-
keeper and slips must expect something every ball, in fact,
the wicket-keeper, whatever the conditions of the wicket,
MUST expect to receive every ball; the wicket-keeper who
assumes that the batsman "must hit this one", may as well
retire from wicket-keeping. You must be on your toes for
every ball, and never once, however long the day, relax your
concentration.

GREATEST PROBLEM

I find a number of young wicket-keepers who say their
greatest problem is seeing the ball all the time when the

batsman is playing his stroke and thus obscuring their view. This is not just a problem for beginners, it is one which never leaves you during your wicket-keeping career. Some batsmen make it far more difficult than others. My greatest headache was keeping to Jack Walsh, the Australian who played in England for Leicestershire. He was a left-hander and seemed to have a double swing. I am sure I let more byes when Jack was batting than any other player, and yet I was doing nothing wrong. Practice for a wicket-keeper in the nets without a batsman is still invaluable provided you have a bowler who can drop the ball on the right spot. I have spent hours in the nets keeping to Tony Lock and Alec Bedser. Tony would put a piece of silver paper down and keep bowling at it. This constant practice teaches you just what the ball is likely to do if the batsman doesn't hit it; experience will teach you what deflections are possible when the batsman gets a touch, but always be ready to go anywhere. If you are standing up on the stumps always be prepared to have to run round the batsman and possibly take a catch in front of the wicket, and watch for a run-out if the batsmen have gone for a quick single. A catch straight up in the air near to the wicket is always the wicket-keeper's. There is nothing more ridiculous in any grade of cricket than when two fielders go for the same catch, collide, and the ball goes down; the spectators enjoy the joke!

IN IT TOGETHER

Always remember that the wicket-keeper and the bowler are in this together. They can work out a combined strategy. I remember the first time I ever kept to Doug Wright, one of the really great leg-spinners. Doug arranged to give me a sign when he was about to bowl his faster ball. Naturally the sign was always varied; otherwise I should have found it a great help the next time I batted against him, but whether you get a sign or not, you must watch the bowler's hand all the time. How silly you look when a leg-break bowler throws up a googly and you go the wrong way. It does happen, of course, even in first-class cricket, and one first-class keeper friend of mine used to lose sleep at night because he seemed quite unable to read one of his team's googly. If you cannot spot what is likely to happen the bowler will be only too pleased to show you his various grips. After all, it is very important to him for you to know; you will help him get a lot more wickets. I remember some uncomfortable moments the first time I kept to Johnny Wardle in trying to pick out his chinaman – the left hander's wrong 'un, but I could tell you almost in my sleep when Alec Bedser was going to bowl an inswinger and when he was going to bowl a leg-cutter. People used to be surprised sometimes that I could bring off a stumping off one of Alec's cutters. It was only because I could tell it was coming before the ball left Alec's hands and I thus had fair warning – perhaps, rather more than the batsman!

I was extremely lucky during my career with Surrey to keep wicket to some great bowlers. Believe me, keeping to Jim Laker was an education and never easy. I let a packet of byes off Jim in one match on a particularly spiteful wicket when he was making the ball do practically everything except talk. Jim had one of the shrewdest cricket brains in the game and we would often have a word as we crossed between overs. I might have been able to have spotted something about the batsman which Jim hadn't seen up to that moment and then, by pre-arrangement, he would bowl a certain type of ball in his next over, and many a time it came off.

A FLAIR FOR IT

What a lucky thing it was for me during the war in Italy when Alec and Eric Bedser suggested that I should take up wicket-keeping because Surrey might be in need of one at the end of the war. What is the first thing a budding wicket-keeper needs? I would say a flair for it – a natural instinct. You cannot make anyone into a 'keeper, but you can develop someone with a bent for it, and who is – and this is vital – READY TO LEARN. When a coach is given a young player who thinks he knows it all, believe me, he soon finds his own interest ebbing. What does the young player need to know? First, the best possible stance, and then the basic principles of movement. As far as the stance is concerned I would stress that he must be absolutely comfortable and nicely balanced. I would recommend feet apart about the width of the shoulders and don't get into the habit when you are crouching, of resting your hands on the ground so that if you took your hands away you would topple over. If I am asked to go and look at a young wicket-keeper, as I often am in my position as Coach to Surrey, I need to watch only about half a dozen balls to make up my mind one way or the other. I watch three things.

1. His position behind the stumps.
2. The placing of his hands.
3. His movements.

Position behind the stumps. It must be one thing or the other – right back or up on the stumps, there is no value in a sort of no-man's land. I have seen wicket-keepers keeping to slow bowlers so far behind the stumps that even if they got the ball in their hands with the batsman out of his ground, they could not reach the stumps without moving their feet towards them. By the time they have done this the batsman is back in his ground and an opportunity which may never occur again has been lost. You must aim to receive the length ball waist-high. If you are keeping to a fast-bowler and in the first over the ball is tending to go over your head . . . move back. If it is coming through ankle high . . . move forward; what the ball is doing is governed to a great extent by the wicket and you won't know the pace of the wicket until you try it. Bowlers vary in their personal feelings. Some fast bowlers get annoyed if they see the wicket-keeper standing right up to the stumps, a position they feel, that suggests that they are not, after all, really fast. Others bowl better if the keeper is on the stumps, but there is nothing brave in standing up to a fast bowler, letting forty byes, and dropping a couple of catches which you would have taken had you been standing in a sensible position. Alec Bedser always liked me up to the stumps and probably bowled that little bit better if I was.

PARAMOUNT IMPORTANCE

The placing of the hands is of paramount importance. Hands should be cupped and the fingers never pointing at the ball. Outstretched fingers in the direction in which the ball is coming are sitting targets to be broken, and in these days when gloves afford such protection, broken fingers are not a sign of bravery but of bad keeping. How different it was in the days of the great Herbert Strudwick whose fingers now have to be seen to be believed. "Struddy" used to practise taking throws with no pads on. He always said that by doing that he made sure he caught them all . . . he didn't want permanently sore shins!

Movements must always be swift but relaxed. Sometimes I've gone out and found myself tense. I have said to myself, "Relax, relax," ride with the ball, with the whole body relaxed . . . don't snatch. If you are naturally right-handed you must get your colleagues to practise throwing at your left hand. Wicket-keeping is certainly a two-handed job. I am sorry to bring out the old chestnut which coaches tell you time and time again whatever the sport . . . Keep your eye on the ball, it is the most vital basic principle in every game, and not least in cricket. It doesn't matter what the batsman's bat is doing. It only matters what the ball is doing. If the batsman plays it be ready to come up to the stumps if you are standing back for a possible run-out. Don't lose interest if the ball is thrown in to the other end – there may be over-throws and in this case it might be flung in to you . . . if you are on your way back to receive the next ball a lucky batsman gets a second innings.

When standing up to the wicket make sure that your left foot is in line with the middle stump and your right foot outside the line of the off-stump, so that you have a clear view of the bowler delivering the ball. This is for a right-hand batsman and the procedure would be reversed for a left-handed batsman. When standing up a wicket-keeper should always try to move towards the wicket, especially on the leg-side. When he sees the ball going down the leg-side to a right-handed batsman he should push off with his right foot and aim to land with his left foot slightly forward of the right, his back then facing fine-leg.

A ball which all wicket-keepers find difficulty in taking is a half-volley outside the off-stump. I have found it easier here to move my right foot backwards, keeping the left still, thus giving me an extra yard in which to take this awkward ball without losing the chance of a stumping.

USE YOUR HANDS

Here is another point worth remembering. Always make a throw-in look as good as possible. If you run to meet a throw even if it is well wide and catch it on the full toss or half-volley it looks a much better throw. The man who has thrown in badly feels much better about it. Never put your pads to it when you could have used your hands. It sets a good wicket-keeper's teeth on edge when he sees both pads used . . . that is small boys' cricket on Clapham Common.

Going back to the stance for a moment I found it very helpful not to crouch when taking fast bowling. If you are in a crouched position before the bowler bowls, you have still got to come up. I always stood with my hands on my knees quite comfortably and found I could move much quicker. Keith Andrew told me that he spotted me doing this very early in his career, followed suit and found it a great benefit. So I pass it on to you for what it is worth.

"Can I practise by myself?" I am often asked. I always reply "Yes" and even when you are at home! Use a chair as a wicket, stand behind it and carry out all your normal movements, and keep on doing it until you do it in your sleep . . .

Cricket—The West Indian Way

by Garfield Sobers

This great West Indian all-rounder has now played in forty-seven Test matches for a batting average of nearly sixty and has played the highest Test innings in history – 365 not out. Sobers has also taken 98 Test wickets and made 54 catches. An elegant stroke-maker Sobers is probably the most attractive player in the world today.

CRICKET in the Caribbean . . . Is it so different from anywhere else in the world? I believe that it is but then I suppose being a West Indian I naturally would. Certainly, I believe that cricket is almost a religion in the Islands especially with the youngsters. It was with me and since I have never had any coaching in my life I suppose it was my instinctive enthusiasm for the game which made me absolutely determined to make a success of my cricket career. So above all else I would say to a young cricketer, "Practise every minute you have to spare". I think I can say that I practised what I preach, for as a boy I have thrown a tennis ball about for as long as eight hours a day. Don't ever be ashamed as a boy of playing cricket with a tennis ball. I found that I knew it would not hurt me and so had no fear. When later on I began playing with a hard ball I had psychologically conditioned myself to have no fear and I was able to apply that feeling because it came naturally when an ordinary cricket ball was being used. A batsman who is expecting all the time to get hurt stands a very good chance of doing so. I have batted against the world's fastest bowlers after coming into first-class cricket in 1953 and was not seriously hit until 1961 when playing for M.C.C. against Oxford University at Lord's. In fact, when I first came into cricket I used to be teased and told that when Miller and Lindwall bowled to me for the first time they would pitch short and knock me down, so to try and give myself confidence against them I used to bat in our nets against the fast bowlers, with no pads or batting gloves or any other form of protection. Believe me you make certain you don't get hit! But I certainly found it a help when I did face the two Australian pace-men for the first time.

If I have had no coaching how did I learn my cricket?

How did I know what to do? The answer to that is by watching great players – three great Barbadians, Everton Weekes, Frankie Worrell, and Roy Marshall; as there were no coaching facilities available to me, I had to watch and absorb the knowledge from what I saw. Speaking of the West Indian difference, I believe, and so it seems do the Australians, that you should try and do something of everything. The theory these days in England is that cricket has become so much a specialist game, that there is no room any more for the all-rounder. I think there is. Take my own case. I began my cricketing career as a left-arm spinner and batted at No. 9. But my batting developed much quicker than my bowling and I think I was wise to work on my batting. In due course I had made quite a number of very high scores and was fairly certain of a place in the West Indies Test side for a season or so, but instead of sitting back and resting on my laurels I started work all over again on my bowling, so that I have now got two strings to my bow instead of one. I think it is essential in any side to be able to bat and bowl. I think that the West Indian cricketer is so keen to bat and bowl that he has tended in his early years to neglect his fielding, a vital omission, which we have had to put right.

One of the most important things at any time in your career is to know what you are doing wrong. Every time you get out, try and think why. If you are getting out in the same way you can probably spot the fault very quickly. When you know what is wrong try and put it right, and this brings me to another very important point. When you have a net what do you do? Do you just get somebody to bowl to you and try and hit him all over the place getting a lot of pleasure out of hitting him hard and often? If you do then you are probably wasting your time. Use net practice to try and correct faults. Try and get the bowler to bowl the sort of ball which is bringing about your downfall in matches, and let him keep bowling it, until in due course you are able to iron out the flaw. There have certainly been flaws in my own batting from time to time and I have quickly got to work on it in this way. After all, you can ask a bowler in the nets to bowl you a particular type of ball . . . you can hardly do this in a match!

The secret of a class batsman is to be able to bat on any wicket and the experience that I have had in the Lancashire League has done more to equip me for top-class cricket than anything else. The wickets there are quite naturally very different from the Test wickets of the world. You have to treat every ball on its merit, which means you can never relax your concentration. This is vital in building any innings. I believe that you should spend the first twenty minutes or so having a good look round at the bowlers and the wicket. That doesn't mean that you don't bother about runs. If you are lucky enough to get six rank bad balls in that time you should be 24 not out! But by looking round I mean you should watch the bowler to see from where he delivers the ball; how he grips it; where the ball leaves his hand, either late or early, and the projection through the air. Some bowlers will give you a good deal more trouble than others. Look how difficult English Test batsmen found Sonny Ramadhin; even now some of the great players could not pick him. I had a lot of trouble when I began with Gupte, the Indian spinner. He used to bowl two types of googlies with an almost identical delivery so that I had to watch the ball rotating in the air to try and pick it out.

I suppose that any shot in any game can be played with perfection only "If" . . . and this is a very big "If" . . . the player is in the right position to play it, so always get into position as quickly as possible. Use your feet . . . and never be afraid to use them . . . they were made to take you from one place to the other, and in cricket, they must take you quickly.

When a bowler is doing all he can to worry you it is often good policy to worry him. If I were batting against a fast bowler on a bad wicket, or on a wicket where he has found a spot, I would move well out of my crease to take guard. After all you are not going to get stumped off a fast bowler and moving to receive the ball a foot or so nearer the bowler can throw him off his length and perhaps upset him completely. Let him see that you are the master.

Similarly, when I am bowling I use the whole width of the crease; the batsman may find difficulty with the ball coming at him from different angles. Never let him settle down into a routine. If you are varying your bowling position – that is the position from where you deliver the ball, it is more profitable to do it gradually, almost so that the batsman hardly notices any difference and is not on his guard.

I have spent a lot of my time on the world's cricket fields fielding in the slips and I would say this. Stay down until the ball is completely played. Remember, it is easier to get up quickly than it is to get down quickly; watch the edge of the bat and not the ball, and never snatch. Let the ball come to you. And finally, do keep yourself fit. Cricket is a game of fast reflexes. If you are fit you move quicker and that quick movement will win matches which would otherwise be lost.

Trevor Bailey

discusses the all-important subject of fielding

The greatest all-rounder in English post-war cricket, Trevor
Bailey has played 61 times for England, performed the hat-
trick against Glamorgan in 1950 and scored 205 for Essex
against Sussex in 1947. He has also taken all ten wickets in
an innings. In addition he has an Amateur Cup Medal as an
inside forward with Walthamstow Avenue. Is now a Director
of Southend United.

A CAPTAIN cannot hope to have a strong batting line-up
without good batsmen, or a penetrating attack without
good bowlers, but he should never rest until he has a competent fielding side. This is merely a matter of ceaseless
practice. You cannot make a class batsman or bowler, but
anyone given the necessary physical co-ordination and the
willingness to work can become a useful fieldsman. Never
was this elementary point more clearly stressed than by the
1955 South African team under Jack Cheetham. They became the best all-round fielding side to visit this country
since the war, simply because they practised so hard and so
often. At the beginning of the tour when I first played against
them, they fielded well, without being exceptional, but by
the end they were brilliant without a weak link. What a
difference it makes if there are no passengers in the field
who have to be hidden as discreetly as possible. Unfortunately there is a tendency to think of fielding as drudgery.
This false idea usually stems from badly organized fielding
practice. Fielding, and fielding practice, should be fun.

Despite its importance, fielding is the least publicized
department of the game, perhaps because there are no
averages to support the value of a brilliant fielder.

However, the fact remains that a team that is outstanding
in the field can transform an ordinary attack into a very
formidable combination.

That old saying, "Hold your catches and win your
matches" remains as true as ever, and catching is of course
the most vital part of fielding. It is distressing to see sloppy
ground fielding and inaccurate throwing, but normally the
outcome is not so painful as the missed catch. Drop a batsman with an average of fifty before he has scored and there
is every chance that this mistake will cost at least fifty runs.

45

No team can afford to squander chances and it is not surprising to find that in nearly all the really big totals the fielding side have put down catches. From this it will be deduced that the most important fielders are those who field in attacking positions close to the bat and snap up those chances, and half chances. The higher the grade of cricket the more players will specialize in these close positions, and with practice obviously the more expert they become. This is particularly true of short leg where in time the fieldsman learns to anticipate a batsman's reaction to a certain type of delivery.

THE SLIPS

Slip is usually the most vital position in the field, as unless the majority of the bowling comes into the bat, he will over the course of a season receive more catches than anyone else.

Life in the slips (when the batsmen are in command) can often be dull, as for long periods of time he may not touch the ball and there is a danger of his allowing his concentration to lapse. This is something he must constantly guard against as this is just the moment when a catch is liable to occur.

First slip should watch the ball from the bowler's hand and I am in favour of second and third doing likewise, although some people maintain that they should watch the bat like gully.

The biggest problem confronting first slip is how fine and how deep to stand. Providing the wicket-keeper is standing back the first problem is largely solved and he has merely to decide on fineness. When the keeper is back I am in favour of first slip standing wide and letting the *gloved* keeper go for everything. On occasions this will lead to a catch bisecting the two of them, but the larger catching area created, more than compensates for this.

It is much more difficult for the slips when the keeper is up at the wicket as he often obscures the ball. When a slow bowler is operating, first slip has to decide whether it will pay greater dividends to come up very close for the edged defensive shot although this means he has little chance of holding on to a mis-slash or a mis-hit. Over the course of a season, the slip who stands straight and deep (to slow bowling) will probably be the most successful. The odd catch will not carry, but he will swallow others that would have been very difficult close.

GULLY

On a wicket that pops gully tends to come in close, but normally he will be close enough to pick up the edged chances but deep enough to hold and to stop cuts. In addition to the catches that may come his way a good gully will save a large number of runs.

On a really good wicket a very deep gully may prove a sound investment. He is largely a defensive fielder, but sometimes he will have the opportunity to catch a full blooded cut.

THE SHORT-LEGS

The best short-legs are to be found in teams that have good off-break and inswing bowlers. Players who field close in the leg trap, and this naturally applies more to when off-spinners rather than inswingers are bowling, must have complete confidence in the bowler or they will not stand close enough. A fieldsman who stands a yard or so from the bat and about square to the wicket must be in considerable physical danger whenever the bowler delivers a long-hop or full-toss. Even when a top-class bowler is operating there is always an element of risk when the batsman chances his arm and swings. From this it will be seen that courage is an essential requisite for a short-leg.

Short-leg should concentrate on the bat and in this way he will on occasions be able to anticipate the stroke.

THE MID POSITIONS

At the present time a ringed field is very often used, especially by medium and slow left-arm bowlers. In a ringed field the players, apart from the one or two close to the wicket attackers, are placed to prevent the ball being hit to the boundary but close enough to stop the single; these are the mid positions.

As the ball is bowled the fielder should walk in. The exact distance he should be from the wicket must depend on the speed of the individual. Sometimes an unwary batsman can be trapped by the fielder going a shade deeper and allowing a run to be stolen in the hope that this will be attempted again when he is closer.

The mid positions include cover which in the past was always occupied by an outstanding fieldsman. Today, because of the increase of inslant bowling it is no longer such a vital spot and often short-extra and short mid-wicket will have more work to do.

Fieldsmen between short extra and short third man must beware of a pronounced clockwise slice which is likely to occur when the ball is hit towards them with a straight or semi-straight bat.

When a slow bowler is operating it often pays for mid-off and mid-on to drop deeper and let short extra and short mid-wicket cut off the pushed single. With nobody back on the boundary the batsman may be tempted to hit the ball back over their heads when a slight error of timing could give them a catch.

THE OUTFIELDERS

This is a broad category as there is obviously a big difference to fielding third man to a fast bowler and deep mid-wicket to an off-spinner when the batsmen are attacking. The former has little likelihood of receiving a catch, while the latter is eagerly waiting. However, the main requirements for all outfielders are the ability to move quickly, to possess a strong accurate return, and to be a safe catch.

The high catch that comes to an outfielder is normally, unless he has to make ground to it, comparatively simple, providing he has the confidence in his own ability which only comes from knowledge gained in practice. The big difference between a close-to-the-wicket catch and the skier is that the former is instinctive while in the latter the fieldsman has time to think. Immediately a fieldsman starts worrying about whether he is going to hold on to the catch, the probability of it being put down is greatly increased.

All outfielders should make sure that the batsmen cannot take more than one when the ball is hit in their region.

Here are some general fielding tips to remember:
(1) Always return the ball to the wicket-keeper unless there is a chance of a run-out at the other end.
(2) Try to throw full tosses into the wicket-keeper's hands just over the top of the stumps: aim for as flat a trajectory as possible.
(3) Don't run with the ball before throwing in as it wastes valuable time.
(4) Most overthrows could be prevented if the appropriate fieldsman backed up.

(5) When stopping a ball try to get as much of your body as possible behind the hands as a second line of defence.

(6) Never snatch at a catch. Let it enter the natural cup formed by the hands and give in the direction the ball is travelling.

(7) Close-to-the-wicket fielders must get down and stay down as the ball is bowled; the others must be moving in.

If you are just a cricket watcher,

Frank Lee, famous Test-Match Umpire, aims to help your watching

Frank Lee was appointed a Test umpire in 1948 and has now umpired over 30 Test matches. As a player he played for Middlesex and Somerset, has scored two centuries in the same match and 141 in the next match. He hit altogether 23 centuries.

Most spectators who watch cricket and especially County cricket have played the game at some time or another. But first-class cricket is naturally more exacting than the game played at week-ends or odd one-day matches, if only for the fact that the players by playing six days a week are generally more proficient. After playing in first-class cricket for over twenty years I found myself, because of the war, playing the game on odd days only. This greatly increased my respect for the week-end Club player because by not constantly playing I found great difficulty in sighting the ball quickly enough at the commencement of my innings, to judge its length and so deal with the bad ball as efficiently as previously. A good batsman in constant practice automatically knows when the ball is in flight, in what way he can best deal with it by moving backwards or forwards. Those playing regularly naturally have a great advantage and for that reason the cricket enthusiast quite rightly expects to see competent performers.

If a spectator can only spare a few days to watch cricket it might be worth his while to study the County fixtures and so see those players whom he feels might make his day more enjoyable. Such batsmen as Peter May, Colin Cowdrey, Ted Dexter, Tom Graveney, and Roy Marshall, to mention only a few, are beautiful stroke makers and a good score by any of these is always worth seeing. On the other hand if one likes to see good bowling then Brian Statham, Freddie Trueman and Tony Lock can usually be relied upon. All spectators enjoy a real needle match and games such as Yorkshire versus Lancashire, Middlesex or Surrey would most likely meet their requirements, while of course one can judge by following the County table which sides are in form, and so make sure of seeing them when they are playing in the vicinity.

The weather and the varying conditions of a pitch often can decide how a match may go, for batsmen cannot be expected to make their usual strokes on a rain-soaked or turning pitch. Of course some followers of cricket remark that they are not certain when they can get to a County game and only attend when they have a few hours to spare, in such cases they then have to take pot luck. There are many points to watch at a cricket match such as bowling, batting, fielding, wicket-keeping, and last but not least, captaincy. I believe that the game can become more interesting for the keen onlooker by occasionally changing his seat, and so obtaining a different viewing point. By sitting square on with the wicket, the onlooker can see far better the length of ball bowled, he can judge possible run-outs and stumpings, and generally be nearer to the game in progress, but by sitting behind the bowler's arm, he can see what use the bowler is making of the ball, by "swing" and "spin", and how the batsmen are combating each and every ball they receive. Should he be, or have been, a bowler himself he can watch every move the bowler makes, his bowling action, his use of the bowling crease, and how he bowls to his field. Likewise, a batting enthusiast can watch the batsmen's footwork and stroke play.

EXPERIENCED PERFORMER

At the start of each innings in first-class cricket the opening bowler has the use of a new ball, and an experienced performer is helped by the shine on the ball, in making it swing late in flight, on or off the pitch. It isn't much use when bowling to a good batsman in making the ball swing too early, but with late swing, and because the ball has more bounce when new, it is naturally more difficult to play, and an opening bowler is more likely to obtain the wickets of good batsmen by the new ball's added speed off the pitch. This is one of the reasons why county sides need batsmen who are specialists in dealing with fast new ball bowlers: and who can, by giving their side a good start, make run getting for the later batsmen far more easy. When bowlers are bowling well, and the pitch is taking spin, those watching behind the bowler's arm can appreciate with added interest the difficulties the batsmen are facing, and can realize that in some circumstances it can be almost a question of survival rather than of making runs. Spectators who become impatient with slow scoring are often those not in the best position to see what the ball is doing, or best qualified to understand the game.

Throughout the years the cricket authorities have made constant alterations that are not always shown in the laws of cricket, but come under the heading of "special regulations for first-class cricket only". When it has been found that the batting or bowling have become too dominant, alterations have been made to adjust the balance. Just after the war with high scoring prevalent, instructions were given to groundsmen to endeavour to make pitches that would help to prevent the many drawn games, and it was felt that the cricket watching public would welcome matches that ended in a definite result. The balance, however, went too far against the batsmen, and because of turning wickets, stroke making naturally became too cautious. In addition, by packing the on side with fielders, fast or spin bowlers made things more and more difficult. Consequently, a special regulation was laid down that bowlers be only allowed five fielders on the on side, with only two of these behind the batting crease. With spinners still having matters too much on their side, groundsmen in recent years have been asked to make faster pitches. These pitches are covered after close of play each day. When heavy rain falls during the playing hours, and the umpires consider that further rain may so affect the pitch as to delay the start next day, they have to instruct the groundsmen to immediately cover the pitch; they then inform the captains and play is called off for that day.

UMPIRE'S DECISION

Instead of the captains deciding when play shall commence or recommence after a stoppage, it is now the umpire's decision. In Test matches the side which is batting can appeal against the light once only in each session of play, and although this has not always been the case in County Cricket, the Advisory County Cricket Committee recommended its adoption at a meeting in November, 1962. Law 30 (bye and leg byes) is very misleading to those that play Club cricket and watch first-class cricket, as there is a different interpretation in the awarding of leg byes. These are allowed in Club cricket unless the umpire considers the batsman has deliberately kicked or kneed the ball away; whereas in first-class cricket the umpire has to decide whether the batsman was making a stroke at the ball with his bat, with the ball coming off his person before awarding leg byes. The Laws of Cricket indicate that the captain of the fielding side may demand a new ball after 200 runs or 65 overs have been bowled, but in first-class cricket nowadays a new ball may only be allowed to the fielding side after 85 overs have been bowled.

The spectator behind the bowler's arm can best appreciate the problems which the l.b.w. law sets the umpire: he has to decide whether the ball pitched on, or to the off side of, the wicket, whether it would have hit the wicket, and whether the part of the batsman's body which it struck was at that instant between wicket and wicket: he must be satisfied about all three before he can give him out. The spectator is as a rule too far away to see or hear the snick or deflection which makes the umpire give a decision against the bowler.

CORRECT GUARD

The elementary business of giving the correct guard to each batsman (from a position directly behind the stumps in order to be in line from wicket to wicket), has at times bewildered me when a batsman has asked for guard from where the bowler delivers, for naturally he cannot so receive the correct guard. This reminds me of the tale of a captain who, while fielding at mid-off remarked to the umpire who had negatived an l.b.w. appeal, "Even I could see from where I am standing that the batsman was out". The umpire was later able to emphasize the point to the captain concerned when asked by him for guard upon coming in to bat, by enquiring, "Shall I give you guard from behind the wicket or from mid-off?".

In first-class cricket the last over before an interval or before close of play is decided by whether or no time has been reached when the umpire, walking at normal pace from his position at square leg, reaches the wicket at what would be the bowler's end.

There are many headaches for umpires that may not be appreciated by the onlooker, such as whether a bowler drags or throws, but with all the snags entailed he is probably enjoying the cricket as much as the spectators, mainly because he has had his share of playing and, I trust, knows his cricket. By first playing in the game he has a better understanding of the feelings of the players and makes allowances accordingly.

Cricket is Such a Game for Nostalgia

By Gordon Ross

THE past, the present, and the future; each has its own specific degree of importance attached to it according to the mood; the cricketer, mellow, perhaps, with many years now long since passed, looks back with a deeper affection than he looks forward. Where will he ever again see the regal majesty of Hammond's cover driving . . . the cunning flight of Hedley Verity, or the machine-like precision of Bradman. Things are not what they used to be – they never were, of course; a golden sunlight seems always to glow with a warmth of affection upon things passed. It rarely appears to shine on the present. As with great musicians, great painters, their greatness is so often reflected only after their death; they know fame posthumously. This, of course, is not true of our contemporary cricketers. We know full well the classical mouldings of a May, a Cowdrey, a Sheppard, or a Dexter, but we still have a hankering for the pleasant days of yesteryear, and in this nostalgic mood, I am looking back upon a dozen innings which created a lasting impression; memorable days in the sun in over thirty years of watching first-class cricket. These twelve innings are not necessarily the finest pieces of cricket I have watched.

SWELTERING DAY

There are bowlers in cricket, too, as Alec Bedser so poignantly points out when he bemoans the fact that the last bowler to receive a knighthood was Francis Drake! Some of Laker's feats which I was privileged to see with my own eyes were almost unbelievable and will never be forgotten. The first time I saw the magnificent Larwood pounding over the hallowed turf at Trent Bridge; the day I saw Bob Wyatt, of all people, receiving the last ball of the match against Somerset at Taunton with Worcester needing six to win, and hitting "Bertie" Buse onto the pavilion roof for victory; an innings of Peter May's of something under a hundred against Derbyshire at the Oval when he hit Cliff Gladwin for two straight sixes into the Members' pavilion – it was all golden cricket. For a variety of reasons, however, I have narrowed this broad canvas to the simple dimensions of a dozen innings – and how difficult it was to do.

The story begins at the Rectory Field, Blackheath, on 9th July, 1932; a sweltering day that seemed to happen so often then, and so rarely now; perhaps, again, it is purely a question of distance lending enchantment. I was there to give wholehearted support to the white horse of Kent, and especially to my two schoolboy heroes, Ames and Freeman. There was always a certain amount of satisfaction for me if Kent lost the toss. I should see Freeman, and to this day I deplore the fact that leg-spinning is a dying art, just as much as Neville Cardus does. On this morning at Blackheath, Surrey duly won the toss and presented me with something of an impasse. What schoolboy didn't want to see Hobbs? – and yet I didn't want him to get too many – and, of course, I wanted Freeman to get him out. The heavens, on this occasion, turned out to be masters of diplomacy in seeking a solution for a tricky problem. Hobbs was caught by Fairservice off Freeman for 18, and as the day ran its course things got better and better despite a stand of 110 by Squires and Shepherd, 171–7, 241–9, and only some Cambridge fellow named F. R. Brown, and Parker, the number 11, to get out – surely easy meat for Freeman, but it was here, on this afternoon at Blackheath, that I saw one of the finest innings I think, to this day, I ever remember.

This fellow from Cambridge – F. R. Brown by name – batted for two hours and ten minutes: the result was four 6s and twenty-one 4s, a last-wicket partnership with Parker of 104, of which Brown made 91, and a score of 168. How often I have thought of this innings in recent years when writing a day's cricket for *The Times* or the *Sunday Times*, and having to describe a full day's play with a score of something like 251 for 8. Brown scored 53 out of 68 in an hour; reached 101 thirty-five minutes later, and put on 50 more in twenty minutes, before dying gloriously with all guns blazing – caught in the shadow of the sightscreen by A. M. Crawley. This was a bitter pill for a young Man of Kent to suffer – Freeman's figures – 4 for 163, but Blackheath has not seen many better innings than this. I wish it was on film for posterity's sake.

THE GREAT MAN

It was a year later, in 1933, and also Kent v. Surrey, again at Blackheath, that I take my second cricketing landmark. It was the first, and, indeed, only time that I saw Jack Hobbs make a hundred. How impossible it seems that the Great Man is eighty years old. This was his 194th century so there were only three more to come. He scored 101 out of an opening stand with Andrew Sandham of 159 in two hours; still the undoubted Master although already in the sunset of a remarkable career. I can now say with pride, "I once saw Jack Hobbs make a hundred".

A highlight of this same season, incidentally, was a last-wicket partnership of 132 for West Indies against Middlesex at Lord's by Valentine and Griffith in fifty-eight minutes – I repeat – fifty-eight minutes. I also saw my first Test match at Lord's with a ticket given to me by the late Rev. F. H. Gillingham, who did much to stimulate and foster my interest in the game; I saw Hedley Verity bowl an under at the Oval – in disgust – when Surrey were batting on after lunch on the second day with a score of over 500!

I have digressed a little from the twelve innings. My third – a Blackheath triumvirate – is a hundred by Frank Woolley – again the first and only one I saw this glorious player make, although I did once see him get a six over slips' heads! Woolley's century on this particular occasion in 1934 forged a magnificent victory for Kent, who had been set to make 414 to win in the last innings and got the runs with four wickets in hand. What a gem of an innings Woolley's was – flowing grace and elegance, no wonder the bowlers were demoralized. This memorable 132 amply fulfilled great expectations. How I should have liked, a fortnight later, to have made the journey to Canterbury to pay tribute to "Tich" Freeman in his benefit match, but academic and other matters deemed otherwise. I am, however, eternally grateful to my friend Robertson-Glasgow for what he did for me in this game. He was stumped Ames bowled Freeman, not once, but twice! As a result I held him in the highest esteem through the years and this respect has never wavered for a moment. After all, many a player did it for me once in a match, but twice was a rare gift from the gods and without much mucking about, too; "Crusoe" scored 5 and 0 – straight to the point, as it were!

SPARKLING DIAMOND

From Frank Woolley the scene moves to Wally Hammond and a Test match against India at the Oval in 1936. With

Stan Worthington of Derbyshire, Hammond added 266 runs from just after lunch until twenty minutes to six. Hammond made 217 and his ovation will remain one of those sporting memories to last a lifetime. He batted, as if with a sword, driving, cutting, with tremendous power. This was a masterpiece of cricket, a sparkling diamond; this was the real Hammond.

From Hammond, on that August afternoon in 1936 – tranquil and unworried days when happiness was not tested to breaking point by the strain of international unrest or rising costs – I move through those last few years of the 'thirties, through the long weary months of war, to a May day in 1948 at Lord's, and to two cricketers who have given me lasting pleasures and a host of memories. Lord's then was a bubbling happy place – these were the halcyon days of the terrible twins – Edrich and Compton. They were the biggest drawing card Lord's has ever had. Taxi drivers in the City have established many a record for the journey when conveying a fare swiftly to Lord's at any time of the day when word has got round that Edrich and Compton were batting. In some respects the particular memory that I have chosen is not a fair reflection of their amazing talents – because it was a massacre, on a wicket pitched unusually close on the "Father Time" side of the ground, but short boundary or not, at one point in their stand of 424 against Somerset, the pair added 209 in seventy minutes – just think of it – two hundred and nine in seventy minutes, of which Compton made 139. The 424 took exactly four hours, Compton 252 not out, and Edrich 168 not out. It beat all third-wicket records in first-class cricket except one of 445 by Carson and Whitelaw for Auckland against Otago at Dunedin in 1937. At their rate of scoring had Mann delayed the Middlesex declaration by about ten minutes, Edrich and Compton would probably have done the trick, but county captains are not expected to carry all world cricketing records about in their head, and in any event, cricket is not played with the idea of setting up personal records – not in England, at any rate. I shall never forget the anguish on Arthur Wellard's face as the ball was sent hurtling up among the grandstand balcony seats, or cracking up against the wooden fence with enough force to have splintered it. Wellard suffered 0 for 158 and didn't bowl badly at that. No doubt one of the umpires heard at close quarters what he thought about it. The rest of us could guess pretty accurately.

Edrich and Compton – magic words they were, and as illustrious in the pages of history as Gilbert and Sullivan.

BRIGHTLY FADES "THE DON"

I am now half-way there – six innings gone – Brown, Hobbs, Woolley, Hammond, Edrich and Compton – six to come. The first, in that same year of 1948 – the fabulous Bradman and his 150 for the Australians against the Gentlemen of England at Lord's – his farewell appearance at Lord's – we were never to see the immortal "Don" in action again at Headquarters. It was said that never once in his glittering career did Bradman throw his wicket away. I shall always believe that he did on this occasion as soon as he reached 150. The Australian score of 610–5 seemed just about right when Bradman was on the rampage, and although Hassett scored a double century not out, this farewell to Bradman was a momentous occasion, the likes of which we shall never see again. The applause, comparable with the affection shown for Sir Malcolm Sargent on the last night of the Proms, was still ringing out after the little man had hurried through a sea of faces in the pavilion and was gone; a cricketing legend was almost complete.

In 1949 I watched another partnership of immense proportions, and I can hardly be expected to forget it since it was by two University players against a county – 429 unbroken between J. G. Dewes and G. H. G. Doggart for Cambridge University against Essex at Fenner's. They broke the English second-wicket record of 398 set up by William Gunn and Arthur Shrewsbury for Nottinghamshire against Sussex in 1890. At the close of play they were only 26 runs short of the world record for this wicket set up by Nimbalkar and Bhandarkar in India during the preceding winter. Although I was not there on the Monday a battery of press cameras was stationed at Fenner's for the possible breaking of the record as well as a goodly sized press contingent, but apparently Insole, the captain, had already declared and had told E. W. Swanton, who happened to be spending the week-end in Cambridge. It was an amazing day and one that Trevor Bailey is likely to long remember but is equally unlikely to record in his final book of memoirs!

From Fenner's in 1949 to Lord's in 1952 and a Test match against India; sixteen years had passed since I saw Hammond's great innings against India at the Oval; now I was to see another classic – Leonard Hutton's 150. After a reasonably cautious beginning, I believe we saw a vintage Hutton. Hutton the perfectionist – ruthless, powerful, a piece of cricket out of the top drawer, the reason why Hutton will always command a place of reverence in Cricket's "Hall of Fame". Lord's, a fine day, and Hutton in full flower was all that any man could ask.

MAY AND GRAVENEY

I am now left with two innings – both double centuries, and both by contemporary players – May and Graveney. I have seen May play many an innings of intrinsic beauty. I shall remember most his 211 against Notts at Trent Bridge in 1954 not only for the content of this innings, but for a rather different reason. A taxi I had ordered failed to turn up at the ground to convey me to the station to catch positively the last train back to London. The alternative was to run for it; this I did, and had I maintained my speed for a mile I should have been the first man to have done the distance under three minutes let alone four. It was a splendid train which stopped at about forty-three stations, and I had just about got my breath back as we rumbled through Willesden. There were moments when it seemed that my life was moving peacefully to its close, but I weathered the storm with the thought of May's batting as inspiration to keep going!

It is at Trent Bridge again that my story closes, the last of the twelve, Tom Graveney's 258 against West Indies in 1957. I am sure when the farseeing planners devised the game of cricket many centuries ago the sort of player they visualized to play and enhance the game was Tom Graveney. In this innings Tom looked the greatest of them all. I have, by necessity, left out dozens of innings of particular merit; many, smaller scores, but representing a courageous fight back against adversity. The indomitable Washbrook when England had been 17–3 against the Australians at Leeds is just one that springs immediately to mind; rich pastures they have been; happy days with lasting friendships made.

Fact and Curiosity

WHEN was cricket first played? This is difficult to answer but Guildford Court proceedings in 1598 show that boys played cricket there some fifty years before that date.

*　　*　　*

A six at cricket was not introduced until 1910 when the Advisory County Cricket Committee recommended an allowance of six runs for hits over the boundary: hitherto, the ball, for a 6, had to be hit right out of the ground.

*　　*　　*

When W. G. Grace played his last first-class match for the Gentlemen of England against Surrey at the Oval in April, 1908, it snowed during the lunch interval.

*　　*　　*

The first record of cricket overseas was a match between the Navy and British Residents in Aleppo, Syria, 1676.

*　　*　　*

At Plymouth in 1867, the Ugly Men played the Handsome Men. The result was a draw!

*　　*　　*

Do you know the origin of the umpire's white coat? It dates back to 1861 when W. G. Armitstead complained that he could not see the bowler's arm when playing for United England against Free Foresters. The umpire was given a white coat.

*　　*　　*

The first match played by an English team overseas took place in Montreal in 1859 between Eleven of England and Twenty-two of Lower Canada.

The first International match was between Eleven of England and Twenty-two of U.S.A. at Hoboken, New York, also in 1859.

* * *

Cricket a peaceful game? Three players were killed following disagreement at a Kent v. Essex match at Tilbury in 1776!

* * *

Not far from Christchurch in New Zealand there was a picturesque little cricket ground, called equally picturesquely, "The Valley of Peace". Because of the beauty of its surroundings? Not a bit of it – because no woman had ever been permitted to set foot on its masculine turf!

* * *

If you are ever counting up the number of ways a batsman can be out at cricket, bear this one in mind. At a match at the Oval in 1870, J. Southerton left his wicket under the impression that he was out, and nothing, not even the decision of the umpires, could induce him to return to the crease. His name appears on the score-sheet – J. Southerton, retired, thinking he was caught, 0.

* * *

Cricket has a special fascination because so much can happen. But how about this, all off one ball. H. Charlwood, playing at the Oval, gave a catch in the deep-field and was dropped. In starting for a third run, he was run out, and the second run was signalled "one short", so that he was missed; made one run, ran one short, and was run out, all in one hit!

* * *

Is it possible to be bowled from behind the stumps at the batsman's end? M. P. Donnelly, the New Zealander, playing for Warwickshire against Middlesex at Lord's in 1948 was hit on the foot by a ball from J. A. Young which bounced over his head. It struck the ground about a foot behind the stumps and came back and hit the wicket.

The explanation for this piece of magic is that the ball landed in a bowler's footmark.

* * *

W. G. Grace was once fielding in a match when the last ball of the day struck the batsman's pads. Nobody appealed for l.b.w. During the evening the batsman told Grace how lucky he was that there had been no appeal, because he was sure he was out. The following morning, before the first ball was bowled, Grace cried, "How's that?" The batsman was given out l.b.w. from the last ball of yesterday! Present laws prevent this sort of thing happening today.

* * *

David Harris of Hambledon, a former cricketer of no mean repute, suffered much from gout in his last few years. When he batted, a great armchair was always brought to the wicket so that, in the words of the day, after the delivery of the ball the hero was able to sit down in his own calm and simple grandeur and repose.

* * *

Body-line bowling is one of cricket's controversial subjects, but it is nothing new. Over a century ago a Mr. Alfred Mynn was so greatly injured by the fast bowling of a Mr. Redgate, that although he battled on and made a century, so serious and severe were his injuries that he was packed up and laid on the roof of a stage-coach.

Women cricketers? Nothing new, really. In 1811 a three-day match between teams of women was played at Newington for 500 Guineas a side.

*   *   *

"Rain stopped play" are familiar words to cricketers, but what about "Swallows stopped play". In a match between Nottinghamshire and Gloucestershire so many swallows flitted across the wicket that play had to be stopped for a time.

*   *   *

Ron Winfield, playing against the Nottingham City Transport, was put on to bowl when the score was 39 for 3. He took six wickets with his first six balls, and caught the last man out off the first ball of the other bowler. Seven balls, seven wickets, from 39 – 3 to 39 all out.

*   *   *

On the last day of a cricket match between Yorkshire and Derbyshire at Dewsbury, the Derbyshire team, with the exception of two players, took the field in lounge suits. Someone had left the taps on in a room over the Derbyshire professionals' dressing room and all the cricketing clothes were ruined. The two players unaffected, Wright and Higson, had spiked shoes, and therefore had to bowl.

*   *   *

Is it possible for a batsman to score four runs when he is sitting in the pavilion having tea? It has happened. Norman Horner, playing for Warwickshire against Oxford University. One of the umpires was convinced over his cup of tea that a stroke by Horner which he had signalled as four byes, was a hit. The scorer, also at the table, was instructed to add four runs to Horner's score.

*   *   *

The strangest game of cricket on record, described at the time as a very singular game of cricket, was played between the Gentlemen of the Hill and the Gentlemen of the Dale at Linsted Park in 1794. Why so strange? It was played from start to finish on horse-back.

* * *

Have you heard of a middle stump being knocked out of the ground and the bails not falling off? It did happen in a match between New South Wales and Victoria on an intensely hot day in Australia. The sun melted the varnish on the bails and they stuck together. Strictly speaking the only decision the umpires could make was "Not out".

* * *

In a five-a-side match between Kent and Sussex over a hundred years ago both sides had one innings, and neither side scored a run. Kent and Sussex all out Nought!

* * *

When cricket was in its infancy in the Fiji Islands two small villages decided to settle a difference by means of a communal duel at cricket. All the available man and boy power of the villages was produced. The match was 50 a side. The 50 fieldsmen took up all imaginable positions round the wicket, some lurking in trees and some crouching on the slanting roofs of thatched houses. So difficult was it to get the ball past this multitude that the batting side of 50 scored only one run. The fielding side, when they batted, could do no better. The result was a tie – One run each!

* * *

How fast does a fast bowler bowl? When C. T. B. Turner, an Australian, was on a visit to this country, he visited the Royal Arsenal at Woolwich where he was asked to bowl through the electric screens in use for measuring the exact velocity of projectiles. It was found that at a certain point half-way between the wickets the rate of Turner's delivery was 81 feet per second, something like 50 miles an hour.

* * *

How far can a cricket ball be driven by a batsman? A cricketer named Ulyett once hit a ball from Manchester to Bradford! Playing for Yorkshire against Lancashire he hit a ball through a carriage window of a passing train. It was recovered in Bradford!

* * *

What is it worth to score a century in a Test match? When Amar Nath became the first Indian to score a century against England in a Test match, Hindu women tore off their jewellery as presents, a millionaire gave him £800, and another presented him with a car.

* * *

Surrey v. Kent matches have brought plenty of thrills over the years, but nothing quite as hectic as their match at Carshalton in July, 1762. The match was brought to a sudden conclusion owing to a dispute concerning the dismissal of a batsman in Surrey's first innings. From words, they came to blows, which occasioned several broken heads, as likewise a challenge between two persons of distinction!

* * *

Just how unlucky can you be in this sometimes tantalizing game of cricket? F. W. Wright, batting for Oxford University against the Gentlemen of the Midland Counties broke his bat as he played the ball. A piece of the bat hit him on the head and dropped onto the wicket.

* * *

Long-stop was once an accepted position in the field. The first wicket-keeper to dispense with a long-stop was H. Phillips, of Sussex, in 1873 in a match against Gloucester. So good was his wicket-keeping that he used no long-stop in Gloucester's second innings.

* * *

One of the oldest cricket bats in existence is said to date from about 1750. It is made in one piece of willow and measures 40½ inches long as compared with the standard 38 inches of today.

* * *

Cricket, the noble game, so termed, perhaps, because the nobility had so much to do with its early roots and growth. In fact cricket contributed to the death of

Frederick Louis, Prince of Wales, son of George II and father of George III. He was a leading patron of the game in the 1730s and 1740s. He received a severe blow on his body at practice in 1750; from this an abscess formed. It burst when he was dancing at Leicester House the following March and killed him.

*   *   *

Originally there were no laws governing the width of a cricket bat, that is until 1774, during a match at Hambledon when Thomas White of Reigate came in to bat with a home-made implement as wide as the wicket. One of the opposing players produced a knife and shaved it down to proper proportions while White stood angrily watching. A new law was at once introduced which limited the maximum width of all bats to four-and-a-half inches.

Surrey very nearly played a match in Paris in 1789 under the sponsorship of the Duke of Dorset, then British Ambassador, but when the Surrey team was assembled at Dover ready to embark, they were met by the Duke fleeing in the opposite direction, from the French Revolution.

*   *   *

Do you know the origin of the now legendary "Ashes"? In

the winter of 1882–83 the Hon. Ivo Bligh took an England team to Australia. Australia won the first Test, but England won the other two and thus secured the rubber. At the end of the third match some ladies burnt a stump, sealed its ashes in an urn, and presented it to the English captain. It remained his property until he died in 1927, when it was bequeathed in his will to M.C.C. The urn now stands at Lord's where it always remains. It does not go to Australia even if they win the Ashes.

* * *

Do cricketers have special fancies for certain grounds? The answer is "Yes". Don Bradman (now Sir Donald) began his career in England with an innings of 236 against Worcestershire at Worcester in 1930. On succeeding tours he also opened with at least a century on the same ground – 206 in 1934, 258 in 1938, and 107 in 1948. His total runs at Worcester, therefore, 807, with an average of 201.75.

* * *

Do you count your own runs when you are batting? W. N. Rose, played for Emmanuel against Caius in July 1881 because Emmanuel were a man short. He hit 415 not out, until that time the highest individual score ever made in any class of cricket. At the end of his innings he told the scorers that he had actually made 416 and that they had missed one of his runs somewhere.

* * *

During last summer when Preston of Essex bowled W. E. Russell of Middlesex at Brentwood one bail travelled a distance of 37 yards. People asked, "Is this a record?" It is not. When R. D. Burrows of Worcester bowled W. Huddleston of Lancashire at Manchester in 1911, one of the bails travelled 67 yards 6 inches.

* * *

The first ever English touring team to visit Australia sailed from Liverpool in the *Great Britain* on October 20th, 1861. The journey took 65 days. Each player was paid £150 plus expenses.

Cricket the noble game? Yet in Stow's Survey of London about 1700 it says, "The lower classes divert themselves at football, wrestling, cudgels, ninepins, shovel-board, cricket, stowball, ringing of bells, quoits, pitching the bar, bull and bear-baitings, throwing at cocks, and lying at ale-houses." Sports of the upper classes included cock-fighting and backgammon!.

*   *   *

If you ever get discouraged when you are going through a bad patch of not making many runs take heart from the fact that your record is unlikely to be as bad as that of G. Deyes playing for Yorkshire in 1907. Here are his scores in 14 consecutive innings – 0, 0, 0 not out, 1, 1 not out, 0, 0, 0, 0, 1 not out, 0, 0, 0, 0 . . . 14 innings – 3 runs!

*   *   *

The origin of the third stump in cricket (originally there were only two) seems to have stemmed from a match in May, 1775, between Five of Hambledon and Five of Kent when "Lumpy" Stevens bowled several successive balls clean through John Small's wicket. It should be observed from the illustration that "Honest Lumpy" has, as was his custom, selected a fine "brow" o'er which to pitch!

Very few batsmen have gone through a career without bagging the traditional pair – o in each innings. Those famous players who have avoided the ignominy include W. G. Grace, J. B. Hobbs, K. S. Ranjitsinhji, H. Sutcliffe, and D. G. Bradman.

* * *

The unusual sight of a father and son batting to the bowling of a father and son was seen in the Derbyshire v. Warwickshire match at Derby in 1922. W. G. and B. W. Quaife, batting to the bowling of W. and R. Bestwick.

* * *

Alec and Eric Bedser are not the only cricketing twins to have played first-class cricket. There was J. S. and W. H. Denton (Northants), A. D. E. and A. E. S. Rippon (Somerset), and F. G. and W. H. Stephens (Warwickshire).

* * *

An England player batted for an hour and thirty-seven minutes against Australia at Adelaide in the winter of 1946–47 before scoring a run. His name? No, it was not Trevor Bailey, it was the usually rapid scorer, Godfrey Evans. Denis Compton, batting at the other end, took most of the bowling.

* * *

The record number of runs scored off a six-ball over is 32. C. Smart hit G. Hill for 6 – 6 – 4 – 6 – 6 – 4 at Cardiff in 1935.

* * *

At Hove, in 1911, E. Alletson, playing for Nottinghamshire against Sussex, recorded the fastest scoring that has ever been seen in cricket. He scored 189 runs out of 227 in 90 minutes, the last 89 runs being scored in 15 minutes and the last 139 in half an hour. Alletson added 152 for the last wicket with W. Riley, his own share being 142.

* * *

C. F. Root held the unique record of playing for England in three Test matches without getting an innings – all against Australia in 1926.

The County Cricket Championship – the oldest cricket competition in the world, is generally accepted as having started in 1873. The nine Counties who competed that year were Derbyshire, Gloucestershire, Kent, Lancashire, Middlesex, Nottinghamshire, Surrey, Sussex and Yorkshire.

*   *   *

Surrey defeated Sussex by an innings and 485 runs at the Oval in 1888 – the greatest victory in County Championship cricket. Surrey scored 698; Sussex 114 and 99.

Cricket Records

*Indicates "Not out" throughout.

INDIVIDUAL TEST INNINGS OF OVER 300 RUNS

365*	G. Sobers	West Indies v. Pakistan (Kingston)	1957–58
364	L. Hutton	England v. Australia (Oval)	1938
337	Hanif Mohammed	Pakistan v. West Indies (Barbados)	1957–58
336*	W. R. Hammond	England v. New Zealand (Auckland)	1932–33
334	D. G. Bradman	Australia v. England (Leeds) ...	1930
325	A. Sandham	England v. West Indies (Kingston)	1929–30
304	D. G. Bradman	Australia v. England (Leeds) ...	1934

FIVE TEST CENTURIES IN CONSECUTIVE INNINGS

E. D. Weekes (West Indies): 141 (Kingston) v. England in 1947–48
128 (New Delhi)
194 (Bombay)
162 and 101 (Calcutta) v. India in 1948–49

HAT-TRICKS IN TEST CRICKET

F. R. Spofforth	Australia v. England (Melbourne)	....	1878–79
W. Bates	England v. Australia (Melbourne)	....	1882–83
J. Briggs	England v. Australia (Sydney)	....	1891–92
G. A. Lohmann	England v. South Africa (Port Elizabeth)	...	1895–96
J. T. Hearne	England v. Australia (Leeds)	....	1899
H. Trumble	Australia v. England (Melbourne)	....	1901–02
H. Trumble	Australia v. England (Melbourne)	....	1903–04
T. J. Matthews†	Australia v. South Africa (Manchester)	...	1912
T. J. Matthews†	Australia v. South Africa (Manchester)	...	1912
M. J. C. Allom	England v. New Zealand (Christchurch)	...	1929–30
T. W. Goddard	England v. South Africa (Johannesburg)	...	1938–39
P. J. Loader	England v. West Indies (Leeds)		1957
L. Kline	Australia v. South Africa (Cape Town)	...	1957–58
W. Hall	West Indies v. Pakistan (Lahore)	....	1958–59
G. Griffin	South Africa v. England (Lord's)	....	1960

† Matthews achieved the "hat-trick" in each innings.

THE LARGEST INNINGS ON RECORD

1107	Victoria v. New South Wales (Melbourne)	....	1926–27
1059	Victoria v. Tasmania (Melbourne)	....	1922–23

THE SMALLEST INNINGS ON RECORD

| 12 | Oxford University v. M.C.C. (Oxford) | 1877 |
| 12 | Northamptonshire v. Gloucestershire (Gloucester) | 1907 |

THESE PLAYERS REPRESENTED TWO COUNTRIES

Amir Elahi	India (1947–48) and Pakistan (1952–53)
J. J. Ferris	Australia (1886–87 to 1890) and England (1891–92)
S. C. Guillen	West Indies (1951–52) and New Zealand (1955–56)
Gul Mahomed	India (1946 to 1952–53) and Pakistan (1956–57)
F. Hearne	England (1888–89) and South Africa (1891 to 1895–96)
A. H. Kardar	India (1946) and Pakistan (1952–53 to 1957–58)
W. E. Midwinter	Australia (1876–77 to 1886–87) and England (1881–82)
F. Mitchell	England (1898–99) and South Africa (1912)
W. L. Murdoch	Australia (1876–77 to 1890) and England (1891–92)
Nawab of Pataudi	England (1932–33 to 1934) and India (1946)
A. E. Trott	Australia (1894–95) and England (1898–99)
S. M. J. Woods	Australia (1888) and England (1895–96)

THE HIGHEST INDIVIDUAL INNINGS

499	Hanif Mohammed: Karachi v. Bahawalpur (Karachi)	1958–59
452*	D. G. Bradman: New South Wales v. Queensland (Sydney)	1929–30
443*	B. B. Nimbalkar: Maharashtra v. Western Indian States (Poona)	1948–49
437	W. H. Ponsford: Victoria v. Queensland (Melbourne)	1927–28
429	W. H. Ponsford: Victoria v. Tasmania (Melbourne)	1922–23
424	A. C. MacLaren: Lancashire v. Somerset (Taunton)	1895

THE HIGHEST NUMBER OF CENTURIES IN AN ENGLISH SEASON

18	D. C. S. Compton (Middlesex)	1947
16	J. B. Hobbs (Surrey)	1925
15	W. R. Hammond (Gloucester)	1938
14	H. Sutcliffe (Yorkshire)	1932

A THOUSAND RUNS DURING MAY

W. G. Grace (Gloucestershire) in 1895 (May 9th to May 30th – 22 days).
13, 103, 18, 25, 288, 52, 257, 73*, 18, 169 – 1016 runs.

W. R. Hammond (Gloucestershire) in 1927 (May 7th to May 31st – 25 days).
27, 135, 108, 128, 17, 11, 99, 187, 4, 30, 83, 7, 192, 14 – 1042 runs.
Hammond scored his 1000th run on May 28th, equalling Grace's record of 22 days.

C. Hallows (Lancashire) in 1928 (May 5th to May 31st – 27 days).
100, 101, 51*, 123, 101*, 22, 74, 104, 58, 34*, 232 – 1000 runs.

THE FASTEST HUNDRED EVER SCORED

100* – 35 mins. P. G. H. Fender (113*) Surrey v. Northants
(Northampton) 1920

HIGHEST NUMBER OF RUNS SCORED IN
A DAY IN ENGLAND

721 – 10   Australians (721) v. Essex at Southend 1948

THE BIG SIX HITTER

W. J. Stewart, playing for Warwickshire v. Lancashire (Blackpool) 1959,
hit 17 sixes – 10 in a first innings of 155 and seven in a second innings
of 125.

THE WORLD RECORD FOR EACH WICKET

1st	555	P. Holmes and H. Sutcliffe: Yorks. v. Essex (Leyton)	1932
2nd	455	B. B. Nimbalkar and K. V. Bhandarkar: Maharashtra v. Western India States (Poona)	1948–49
3rd	445	P. E. Whitelaw and W. N. Carson: Auckland v. Otago (Dunedin)	1936–37
4th	577	Gul Mahomed and V. S. Hazare: Baroda v. Holkar (Baroda)	1946–47
5th	405	S. G. Barnes and D. G. Bradman: Australia v. England (Sydney)	1946–47
6th	487*	G. Headley and C. C. Passailaigue: Jamaica v. Tennyson's XI (Kingston)	1931–32
7th	347	D. Atkinson and C. Depeiza: West Indians v. Australia (Barbados)	1954–55
8th	433	V. T. Trumper and A. Sims: Australians v. Canterbury (Christchurch)	1913–14
9th	283	J. Chapman and A. R. Warren: Derby v. Warwicks. (Blackwell)	1910
10th	307	A. F. Kippax and J. E. H. Hooker: N.S.W. v. Victoria (Melbourne)	1928–29

Australian batsmen hold three records, English, West Indian and
Indian batsmen two each and New Zealand batsmen one.

MOST NUMBER OF WICKETS IN AN ENGLISH SEASON

	Season	Balls in an over	Overs	Mdns.	Runs	Wkts.	Avge.
A. P. Freeman	1928	(6–ball)	1976.1	423	5489	304	18.05
A. P. Freeman	1933	(6–ball)	2039	651	4549	298	15.26
T. Richardson	1895	(5–ball)	1690.1	463	4170	290	14.37
C. T. B. Turner	1888	(4–ball)	2427.2	1127	3307	283	11.68
A. P. Freeman	1931	(6–ball)	1618	360	4307	276	15.60
A. P. Freeman	1930	(6–ball)	1914.3	472	4632	275	16.84
T. Richardson	1897	(5–ball)	1603.4	495	3945	273	14.45
A. P. Freeman	1929	(6–ball)	1670.5	381	4879	267	18.27
W. Rhodes	1900	(6–ball)	1553	455	3606	261	13.81
J. T. Hearne	1896	(5–ball)	2003.1	818	3670	257	14.28
A. P. Freeman	1932	(6–ball)	1565.5	404	4149	253	16.39
W. Rhodes	1901	(6–ball)	1565	505	3797	251	15.12

HOW FAR CAN A BAIL TRAVEL?

The distances which a bail has travelled after a bowler has clean-bowled a batsman are sometimes almost incredible, and there are a number of cases of over 50 yards. The longest distances are:

yds. ins.

67	6	by R. D. Burrows in bowling W. Huddleston: Worcestershire v. Lancashire (Manchester)	1911
66	0	by H. Larwood in bowling G. W. Martin: M.C.C. v. Tasmania (Launceston)	1928–29
64	6	by R. D. Burrows in bowling A. C. MacLaren: Worcestershire v. Lancashire (Manchester)	1901
63	6	by A. Mold in bowling G. A. Lohmann: Lancashire v. Surrey (Oval)	1896

Season	Visiting Captains	Won by Eng.	Aust.	Drawn	Total
1876–77	J. Lillywhite (E)	1	1	—	2
1878–79	Lord Harris (E)	—	1	—	1
1880	W. L. Murdoch (A)	1	—	—	1
1881–82	A. Shaw (E)	—	2	2	4
1882	W. L. Murdoch (A)	—	1	—	1
1882–83	Hon. Ivo Bligh (E)	2	2	—	4
1884	W. L. Murdoch (A)	1	—	2	3
1884–85	A. Shrewsbury (E)	3	2	—	5
1886	H. J. H. Scott (A)	3	—	—	3
1886–87	A. Shrewsbury (E)	2	—	—	2
1887–88	W. W. Read (E)	1	—	—	1
1888	P. S. McDonnell (A)	2	1	—	3
1890	W. L. Murdoch (A)	2	—	—	2
1891–92	W. G. Grace (E)	1	2	—	3
1893	J. McC. Blackham (A)	1	—	2	3
1894–95	A. E. Stoddart (E)	3	2	—	5
1896	G. H. S. Trott (A)	2	1	—	3
1897–98	A. E. Stoddart (E)	1	4	—	5
1899	J. Darling (A)	—	1	4	5
1901–02	A. C. MacLaren (E)	1	4	—	5
1902	J. Darling (A)	1	2	2	5
1903–04	P. F. Warner (E)	3	2	—	5
1905	J. Darling (A)	2	—	3	5
1907–08	A. O. Jones (E)	1	4	—	5
1909	M. A. Noble (A)	1	2	2	5
1911–12	J. W. H. T. Douglas (E)	4	1	—	5
1912	S. E. Gregory (A)	1	—	2	3
1920–21	J. W. H. T. Douglas (E)	—	5	—	5
1921	W. W. Armstrong (A)	—	3	2	5
1924–25	A. E. R. Gilligan (E)	1	4	—	5
1926	H. L. Collins (A)	1	—	4	5
1928–29	A. P. F. Chapman (E)	4	1	—	5
1930	W. M. Woodfull (A)	1	2	2	5
1932–33	D. R. Jardine (E)	4	1	—	5
1934	W. M. Woodfull (A)	1	2	2	5
1936–37	G. O. Allen (E)	2	3	—	5
1938	D. G. Bradman (A)	1	1	2	4
1946–47	W. R. Hammond (E)	—	3	2	5
1948	D. G. Bradman (A)	—	4	1	5
1950–51	F. R. Brown (E)	1	4	—	5
1953	A. L. Hassett (A)	1	—	4	5
1954–55	L. Hutton (E)	3	1	1	5
1956	I. W. Johnson (A)	2	1	2	5

1958–59	P. B. H. May (E)	—	4	1	5
1961	R. Benaud (A)	1	2	2	5
1962–63	E. R. Dexter (E)	1	1	3	5

In Australia	39	54	9	102
In England	25	23	38	86
Totals	64	77	47	188

GROUNDS

England – The Oval (22), Lord's (20), Old Trafford (18), Headingley (12), Trent Bridge (10), Edgbaston (3), Bramall Lane (1).

Australia – Melbourne (38), Sydney (38), Adelaide (18), Brisbane (8).

SOUTH AFRICA

Season	Visiting Captains	Won by Eng.	S.A.	Drawn	Total
1888–89	C. Aubrey-Smith (E)	2	—	—	2
1891–92	W. W. Read (E)	1	—	—	1
1895–96	Lord Hawke (E)	3	—	—	3
1898–99	Lord Hawke (E)	2	—	—	2
1905–06	P. F. Warner (E)	1	4	—	5
1907	P. W. Sherwell (S.A.)	1	—	2	3
1909–10	H. D. G. Leveson-Gower (E)	2	3	—	5
1912	F. Mitchell (S.A.)	3	—	—	3
1913–14	J. W. H. T. Douglas (E)	4	—	1	5
1922–23	F. T. Mann (E)	2	1	2	5
1924	H. W. Taylor (S.A.)	3	—	2	5
1927–28	R. T. Stanyforth (E)	2	2	1	5
1929	H. G. Deane (S.A.)	2	—	3	5
1930–31	A. P. F. Chapman (E)	—	1	4	5
1935	H. F. Wade (S.A.)	—	1	4	5
1938–39	W. R. Hammond (E)	1	—	4	5
1947	A. Melville (S.A.)	3	—	2	5
1948–49	F. G. Mann (E)	2	—	3	5
1951	A. D. Nourse (S.A.)	3	1	1	5
1955	J. E. Cheetham (S.A.)	3	2	—	5
1956–57	P. B. H. May (E)	2	2	1	5
1960	D. J. McGlew (S.A.)	3	—	2	5

In South Africa	24	13	16	53
In England	21	4	16	41
Totals	45	17	32	94

GROUNDS

England — Lord's (9), The Oval (9), Headingley (8), Old Trafford (7), Edgbaston (3), Trent Bridge (5).

South Africa — Port Elizabeth (5), Capetown (14), Johannesburg (21), Durban (13).

WEST INDIES

Season	Visiting Captains	Won by Eng.	W.I.	Drawn	Total
1928	R. K. Nunes (W.I.)	3	—	—	3
1929–30	Hon. F. S. G. Calthorpe (E)	1	1	2	4
1933	G. C. Grant (W.I.)	2	—	1	3
1934–35	R. E. S. Wyatt (E)	1	2	1	4
1939	R. S. Grant (W.I.)	1	—	2	3
1947–48	G. O. Allen (E)	—	2	2	4
1950	J. D. Goddard (W.I.)	1	3	—	4
1953–54	L. Hutton (E)	2	2	1	5
1957	J. D. Goddard (W.I.)	3	—	2	5
1959–60	P. B. H. May (E)	1	—	4	5
1963	F. M. Worrell (W.I.)	1	3	1	5
	In West Indies	5	7	10	22
	In England	11	6	6	23
	Totals	16	13	16	45

GROUNDS
England   – Lord's (6), The Oval (6), Old Trafford (5), Headingley
              (2), Edgbaston (2), Trent Bridge (2).
West Indies–Bridgetown (5), Port of Spain (6), Georgetown (5), King-
              ston (6).

NEW ZEALAND

Season	Visiting Captains	Won by Eng.	N.Z.	Drawn	Total
1929–30	A. H. H. Gilligan (E)	1	—	3	4
1931	T. C. Lowry (N.Z.)	1	—	2	3
1932–33	D. R. Jardine (E)	—	—	2	2
1937	M. L. Page (N.Z.)	1	—	2	3
1946–47	W. R. Hammond (E)	—	—	1	1
1949	W. A. Hadlee (N.Z.)	—	—	4	4
1950–51	F. R. Brown (E)	1	—	1	2
1954–55	L. Hutton (E)	2	—	—	2
1958	J. R. Reid (N.Z.)	4	—	1	5
1958–59	P. B. H. May (E)	1	—	1	2
1962–63	E. R. Dexter (E)	3	—	—	3
	In New Zealand	8	—	8	16
	In England	6	—	9	15
	Totals	14	—	17	31

GROUNDS
England   – Lord's (4), The Oval (4), Old Trafford (4), Headingley
              (2), Edgbaston (1).
New Zealand – Christchurch (5), Wellington (2), Auckland (5), Dune-
              din (1).

INDIA

Season	Visiting Captains	Won by Eng.	India	Drawn	Total
1932	C. K. Nayudu (I)	1	—	—	1
1933–34	D. R. Jardine (E)	2	—	1	3
1936	Maharaj Kumar of Viziana-gram (I)	2	—	1	3
1946	Nawab of Pataudi (I)	1	—	2	3
1951–52	N. D. Howard (E)	1	1	3	5
1952	V. S. Hazare (I)	3	—	1	4
1959	D. K. Gaekwad (I)	5	—	—	5
1961–62	E. R. Dexter (E)	—	2	3	5
	In India	3	3	7	13
	In England	12	—	4	16
	Totals	15	3	11	29

GROUNDS

England – Lord's (5), The Oval (4), Old Trafford (4), Headingley (2), Trent Bridge (1).

India – Bombay (3), Calcutta (3), Madras (3), New Delhi (2), Kanpur (2).

PAKISTAN

Season	Visiting Captains	Won by Eng.	Pak.	Drawn	Total
1954	A. H. Kardar (P)	1	1	2	4
1961–62	E. R. Dexter (E)	1	—	2	3
1962	J. Burki (P)	4	—	1	5
	In Pakistan	1	—	2	3
	In England	5	1	3	9
	Totals	6	1	5	12

GROUNDS

England – Lord's (2), Trent Bridge (2), Old Trafford (1), Oval (2), Edgbaston (1), Headingley (1).

Pakistan – Lahore (1), Dacca (1), Karachi (1).

INTERNATIONAL TOURS

1963–64	South Africa to Australia
1964	Australia to England
1964–65	M.C.C. to South Africa
1965	New Zealand to England

78

1965–66	M.C.C. to Australia
1966	South Africa to England
1967	India to England
1967–68	M.C.C. to West Indies
1968	Australia to England
1968–69	M.C.C. to South Africa
1969	Pakistan to England
1970	South Africa to England
1970–71	M.C.C. to Australia
1971	West Indies to England
1971–72	M.C.C. to India and Pakistan
1972	New Zealand to England
1973	Australia to England
1973–74	M.C.C. to South Africa
1974	India to England
1974–75	M.C.C. to Australia
1975	Pakistan to England
1976	South Africa to England
1976–77	M.C.C. to West Indies
1977	Australia to England
1977–78	M.C.C. to South Africa
1978	West Indies to England

TEST MATCHES BETWEEN THE OTHER COUNTRIES

	Pl.	Aus. won	S.A. won	W.I. won	N.Z. won	India won	Pak. won	Dr. Drn.
Australia v. South Africa	39	27	3					9
Australia v. West Indies	15	11		2				2
Australia v. New Zealand	1	1			0			0
Australia v. India	13	8				1		4
Australia v. Pakistan	4	2					1	1
S. Africa v. New Zealand	9		7		0			2
West Indies v. N. Zealand	6			4	1			1
West Indies v. India	15			5		0		10
West Indies v. Pakistan	8			4			3	1
New Zealand v. India	5				0	2		3
New Zealand v. Pakistan	3				0		2	1
India v. Pakistan	10					2	1	7

DERBYSHIRE

Highest Inngs. Totals: For ... 645 v. Hampshire (Derby) ... 1898
Agst... 662 by Yorkshire (Chesterfield) 1898
Lowest Inngs. Totals: For ... 16 v. Nottinghamshire (Nottingham) 1879
Agst... 23 by Hampshire (Burton)... 1958
Highest Indiv. Inngs.: For ... 274 G. Davidson v. Lancashire (Manchester) 1896
Agst... 343* P. A. Perrin for Essex (Chesterfield) 1904
Most runs in a season   2165 (av. 48.11) D. B. Carr 1959
runs in a career   20516 (av. 31.41) D. Smith 1927–52
100s in a season   6 by L. F. Townsend 1933
100s in a career   30 by D. Smith 1927–52
wkts. in a season   168 (av. 19.55) T. B. Mitchell ... 1935
wkts. in a career   1670 (av. 17.11) H. L. Jackson 1947–63

RECORD WICKET STANDS

1st 322   H. Storer & J. Bowden v. Essex (Leyton) 1929
2nd 349   C. S. Elliott & J. D. Eggar v. Nottinghamshire (Nottingham) 1947
3rd 246   J. Kelly & D. B. Carr v. Leicestershire (Chesterfield) 1957
4th 328   P. Vaulkhard & D. Smith v. Nottinghamshire (Nottingham) 1946
5th 191   A. G. Slater & A. Morton v. Hampshire (Basingstoke) 1914
6th 212   G. M. Lee & T. S. Worthington v. Essex (Chesterfield) 1932
7th 241* G. H. Pope & A. E. G. Rhodes v. Hampshire (Portsmouth) 1948
8th 182   A. H. M. Jackson & W. Carter v. Leicestershire (Leicester) 1922
9th 283   J. Chapman & A. R. Warren v. Warwickshire (Blackwell) 1910
10th 93   J. Humphries & J. Horsley v. Lancashire (Derby) 1914

ESSEX

Highest Inngs. Totals:	For ...	692 v. Somerset (Taunton) ...	1895
	Agst...	803–4d by Kent (Brentwood)	1934
Lowest Inngs. Totals:	For ...	30 v. Yorkshire (Leyton)......	1901
	Agst...	31 (on two occasions)......1914 & 1935	

Highest Indiv. Inngs.: For ... 343* P. A. Perrin v. Derby-
shire (Chesterfield) 1904
Agst... 332 W. H. Ashdown for Kent
(Brentwood) 1934

Most runs in a season	2308 (av. 56.29) J. O'Connor	1934
runs in a career	29162 (av. 36.18) P. A. Perrin 1896–1928	
100s in a season	9 by J. O'Connor (1934) & D. J. Insole	1955
100s in a career	71 by J. O'Connor	1921–39
wkts. in a season	172 (av. 27.13) T. P. B. Smith......	1947
wkts. in a career	1611 (av. 26.26) T. P. B. Smith......	1929–51

RECORD WICKET STANDS

1st	270	A. V. Avery & T. C. Dodds v. Surrey (Oval) ...	1946
2nd	294	A. V. Avery & P. A. Gibb v. Northampton (Northampton)	1952
3rd	343	P. A. Gibb & R. Horsfall v. Kent (Blackheath)...	1951
4th	298	A. V. Avery & R. Horsfall v. Worcestershire (Clacton)..	1948
5th	287	C. T. Ashton & J. O'Connor v. Surrey (Brentwood)	1934
6th	206	J. W. H. T. Douglas & J. O'Connor v. Gloucestershire (Cheltenham)	1923
	206	B. R. Knight & R. A. G. Luckin v. Middlesex (Brentwood)	1962
7th	261	J. W. H. T. Douglas & J. Freeman v. Lancashire (Leyton)	1914
8th	263	D. R. Wilcox & R. M. Taylor v. Warwickshire (Southend)	1946
9th	251	J. W. H. T. Douglas & S. N. Hare v. Derbyshire (Leyton)	1921
10th	218	F. H. Vigar & T. P. B. Smith v. Derbyshire (Chesterfield)	1947

GLAMORGAN

Highest Inngs. Totals: For ... 587–8d v. Derbyshire (Cardiff) 1951
Agst... 653–6d by Gloucestershire
(Bristol) 1928
Lowest Inngs. Totals: For ... 22 v. Lancashire (Liverpool) 1924
Agst... 35 by Sussex (Horsham)...... 1946
Highest Indiv. Inngs.: For ... 287* E. Davies v. Gloucester-
shire (Newport) 1939
Agst... 302* W. R. Hammond for
Glos. (Bristol) 1934
Most runs in a season 2071 (av. 49.30) W. G. A. Parkhouse 1959
runs in a career 26104 (av. 27.82) E. Davies............ 1924–54
100s in a season 7 by W. G. A. Parkhouse......... 1950
100s in a career 32 by W. G. A. Parkhouse......... 1948–63
wkts. in a season 176 (av. 17.34) J. C. Clay 1937
wkts. in a career 1460 (av. 23.32) J. Mercer............ 1922–39

RECORD WICKET STANDS

1st 274 E. Davies & A. H. Dyson v. Leicestershire (Leicester) 1937
2nd 238 A. Jones & A. R. Lewis v. Sussex (Hastings) 1962
3rd 313 E. Davies & W. E. Jones v. Essex (Brentwood)... 1948
4th 263 G. Lavis & C. Smart v. Worcestershire (Cardiff) 1934
5th 264 M. Robinson & S. W. Montgomery v. Hampshire
(Bournemouth) 1949
6th 230 W. E. Jones & B. L. Muncer v. Worcestershire
(Worcester)....................................... 1953
7th 195* W. Wooller & W. E. Jones v. Lancashire (Liverpool) 1947
8th 202 D. Davies & J. J. Hills v. Sussex (Eastbourne)...... 1928
9th 203* J. J. Hills & J. C. Clay v. Worcestershire (Swansea) 1929
10th 131* C. Smart & W. D. Hughes v. South Africans
(Cardiff)... 1935

GLOUCESTERSHIRE

Highest Inngs. Totals: For ... 653–6d v. Glamorgan (Bristol)   1928
                 Agst... 774–7d by Australians (Bristol)   1948
Lowest Inngs. Totals: For ... 17 v. Australians (Cheltenham)   1896
                 Agst... 12 by Northamptonshire
                       (Gloucester)   1907
Highest Indiv. Inngs.: For ... 318* W. G. Grace v. Yorkshire
                       (Cheltenham)   1876
                 Agst... 296 A. O. Jones for Notts.
                       (Nottingham)   1903
Most runs in a season   2860 (av. 69.75) W. R. Hammond...   1933
     runs in a career   33664 (av. 57.05) W. R. Hammond...   1920–51
     100s in a season   13 by W. R. Hammond   1938
     100s in a career   113 by W. R. Hammond   1920–51
     wkts. in a season   222 (av. 16.80 and 16.37) T. W.
                        Goddard ....1937 & 1947
     wkts. in a career   3171 (av. 19.43) C. W. L. Parker ... 1903–35

RECORD WICKET STANDS
   1st   395   D. M. Young & R. B. Nicholls v. Oxford Univ.
               (Oxford)   1962
   2nd   256   C. T. M. Pugh & T. W. Graveney v. Derbyshire
               (Chesterfield)   1960
   3rd   336   W. R. Hammond & B. H. Lyon v. Leicestershire
               (Leicester)   1933
   4th   321   W. R. Hammond & W. L. Neale v. Leicestershire
               (Gloucester)   1937
   5th   261   W. G. Grace & W. O. Moberley v. Yorkshire
               (Cheltenham)   1876
   6th   320   G. L. Jessop & J. H. Board v. Sussex (Hove)......   1902
   7th   248   W. G. Grace & E. L. Thomas v. Sussex (Hove)...   1896
   8th   239   W. R. Hammond & A. E. Wilson v. Lancashire
               (Bristol)   1938
   9th   193   W. G. Grace & S. A. P. Kitcat v. Sussex (Bristol)   1896
  10th   131   W. R. Gouldsworthy & J. G. Bessant v. Somerset
               (Bristol)   1923

HAMPSHIRE

Highest Inngs. Totals: For ... 672–7d v. Somerset (Taunton)   1899
  Agst... 742 by Surrey (Oval)   1909
Lowest Inngs. Totals: For ... 15 v. Warwickshire (Birmingham)   1922
  Agst... 32 by Kent (Southampton)...   1952
Highest Indiv. Inngs.: For ... 316 R. H. Moore v. Warwickshire (Bournemouth)   1937
  Agst... 302* P. Holmes for Yorkshire (Portsmouth)   1920
Most runs in a season   2854 (av. 79.27) C. P. Mead   1928
  runs in a career   48892 (av. 48.84) C. P. Mead 1905–36
  100s in a season   12 by C. P. Mead   1928
  100s in a career   138 by C. P. Mead 1905–36
  wkts. in a season   190 (av. 15.61) A. S. Kennedy ...   1922
  wkts. in a career   2549 (av. 21.16) A. S. Kennedy ... 1907–36

RECORD WICKET STANDS

1st	249	R. E. Marshall & J. R. Gray v. Middlesex (Portsmouth)	1960
2nd	321	G. Brown & E. I. M. Barrett v. Gloucestershire (Southampton)	1920
3rd	344	C. P. Mead & G. Brown v. Yorkshire (Portsmouth)	1927
4th	259	C. P. Mead & Hon. L. H. Tennyson v. Leicestershire (Portsmouth)	1921
5th	235	G. Hill & D. F. Walker v. Sussex (Portsmouth)...	1937
6th	411	R. M. Poore & E. G. Wynyard v. Somerset (Taunton)	1899
7th	325	G. Brown & C. H. Abercrombie v. Essex (Leyton)	1913
8th	178	C. P. Mead & C. P. Brutton v. Worcestershire (Bournemouth)	1925
9th	230	D. Livingstone & A. T. Castell v. Surrey (Southampton)	1962
10th	192	A. Bowell & W. H. Livsey v. Worcestershire (Bournemouth)	1921

Highest Inngs. Totals:	For ...	803–4d v. Essex (Brentwood)	1934
	Agst...	676 by Australians (Canterbury)	1921
Lowest Inngs. Totals:	For ...	18 v. Sussex (Gravesend)......	1867
	Agst...	16 by Warwickshire (Tonbridge)	1913
Highest Indiv. Inngs.:	For ...	332 W. H. Ashdown v. Essex (Brentwood)	1934
	Agst...	344 W. G. Grace for M.C.C. (Canterbury)	1876
Most runs in a season		2894 (av. 59.06) F. E. Woolley	1928
runs in a career		48483 (av. 42.05) F. E. Woolley	1906–18
100s in a season		10 by F. E. Woolley ....1928 & 1934	
100s in a career		112 by F. E. Woolley	1906–38
wkts. in a season		262 (av. 14.74) A. P. Freeman......	1933
wkts. in a career		3359 (av. 14.45) A. P. Freeman......	1914–36

RECORD WICKET STANDS

1st	283	A. E. Fagg & P. R. Sunnucks v. Essex (Colchester)	1938
2nd	352	W. H. Ashdown & F. E. Woolley v. Essex (Brentwood)	1934
3rd	321*	A. Hearne & J. R. Mason v. Nottinghamshire (Nottingham)	1899
4th	297	H. T. W. Hardinge & A. P. F. Chapman v. Hampshire (Southampton)	1926
5th	277	F. E. Woolley & L. E. G. Ames v. New Zealanders (Canterbury)	1931
6th	284	A. P. F. Chapman & G. B. Legge v. Lancashire (Maidstone)	1927
7th	248	A. P. Day & E. Humphreys v. Somerset (Taunton)	1908
8th	157	A. L. Hilder & C. Wright v. Essex (Gravesend)...	1924
9th	161	B. R. Edrich & F. Ridgway v. Sussex (Tunbridge Wells)	1949
10th	235	F. E. Woolley & A. Fielder v. Worcestershire (Stourbridge)	1909

Highest Inngs. Totals: For ... 801 v. Somerset (Taunton) ... 1895
Agst... 634 by Surrey (Oval) 1895
Lowest Inngs. Totals: For ... 25 v. Derbyshire (Manchester) 1871
Agst... 22 by Glamorgan (Liverpool) 1924
Highest Indiv. Inngs.: 424 A. C. MacLaren v. Somerset
(Taunton)..................... 1895
Agst... 315* T. Hayward for Surrey
(Oval) 1898
Most runs in a season 2633 (av. 56.02) J. T. Tyldesley ... 1901
runs in a career 32267 (av. 41.68) J. T. Tyldesley... 1895–1923
100s in a season 11 by C. Hallows.................. 1928
100s in a career 91 by E. Tyldesley 1909–36
wkts. in a season 198 (av. 18.55) E. A. McDonald... 1925
wkts. in a career 1722 (av. 15.37) J. Briggs............1879–1900

RECORD WICKET STANDS

1st   368   A.·C. MacLaren & R. H. Spooner v. Gloucestershire (Liverpool) 1903
2nd 371   F. Watson & E. Tyldesley v. Surrey (Manchester) 1928
3rd 306   E. Paynter & N. Oldfield v. Hampshire (Southampton) 1938
4th 324   A. C. MacLaren & J. T. Tyldesley v. Nottinghamshire (Nottingham) 1904
5th 235* N. Oldfield & A. E. Nutter v. Nottinghamshire
(Manchester) 1939
6th 278   J. Iddon & H. R. W. Butterworth v. Sussex
(Manchester) 1932
7th 245   A. H. Hornby & J. Sharp v. Leicestershire
(Manchester) 1912
8th 150   A. Ward & C. R. Hartley v. Leicestershire
(Leicester) 1900
9th 142   L. O. S. Poidevin & A. Kermode v. Sussex (Eastbourne) 1907
10th 173   J. Briggs & R. Pilling v. Surrey (Liverpool)......... 1885

LEICESTERSHIRE

Highest Inngs. Totals: For ... 701–4d v. Worcestershire (Worcester) 1906

Agst... 739–7d by Nottinghamshire (Nottingham) 1903

Lowest Inngs. Totals: For ... 25 v. Kent (Leicester) 1912

Agst... 35 by Northants (Northampton) 1907

Highest Indiv. Inngs.: For ... 252* S. Coe v. Northants (Leicester)..................... 1914

Agst... 341 G. H. Hirst for Yorkshire (Leicester)..................... 1905

Most runs in a season   2446 (av. 52.04) L. G. Berry 1937

runs in a career   30106 (av. 30.53) L. G. Berry 1924–51

100s in a season   7 by L. G. Berry (1937) & W. Watson 1959

100s in a career   45 by L. G. Berry 1924–51

wkts. in a season   170 (av. 18.96) J. E. Walsh 1948

wkts. in a career   2130 (av. 23.19) W. E. Astill 1906–39

RECORD WICKET STANDS

1st 380 C. J. B. Wood & H. Whitehead v. Worcestershire (Worcester).. 1906

2nd 287 W. Watson & A. Wharton v. Lancashire (Leicester) 1961

3rd 316* W. Watson & A. Wharton v. Somerset (Taunton) 1961

4th 270 C. S. Dempster & G. S. Watson v. Yorkshire (Hull) 1937

5th 226* R. MacDonald & F. Geeson v. Derbyshire (Glossop) 1901

6th 262 A. T. Sharp & G. H. S. Fowke v. Derbyshire (Chesterfield) 1911

7th 194 W. W. Odell & H. Whitehead v. Essex (Leicester) 1905

8th 150 G. Geary & T. E. Sidwell v. Surrey (Oval)......... 1926

9th 160 W. W. Odell & R. T. Crawford v. Worcestershire (Leicester) 1902

10th 157 W. E. Astill & W. H. Marlow v. Gloucestershire (Cheltenham) 1933

MIDDLESEX

Highest Inngs. Totals: For ... 642–3d v. Hampshire (South-
ampton) 1923
Agst... 665 by West Indians (Lord's) 1939
Lowest Inngs. Totals: For ... 20 v. M.C.C. (Lord's)......... 1864
Agst... 31 by Gloucestershire (Bristol) 1924
Highest Indiv. Inngs.: For ... 331* J. D. Robertson v. Worcestershire (Worcester) ... 1949
Agst... 316* J. B. Hobbs for Surrey
(Lord's) 1926
Most runs in a season 2650 (av. 85.48) W. J. Edrich 1947
runs in a career 40302 (av. 49.81) E. Hendren 1907–37
100s in a season 13 by D. C. S. Compton 1947
100s in a career 119 by E. Hendren 1907–37
wkts. in a season 158 (av. 14.63) F. J. Titmus 1955
wkts. in a career 2133 (av. 17.94) J. T. Hearne 1888–1923

RECORD WICKET STANDS

1st 310 J. D. Robertson & S. M. Brown v. Nottinghamshire (Lord's) 1947
2nd 380 F. A. Tarrant & J. W. Hearne v. Lancashire
(Lord's) 1914
3rd 424* W. J. Edrich & D. C. S. Compton v. Somerset
(Lord's) 1948
4th 325 J. W. Hearne & E. Hendren v. Hampshire (Lord's) 1919
5th 338 R. S. Lucas & T. C. O'Brien v. Sussex (Hove)... 1895
6th 212 J. H. A. Hulme & G. O. Allen v. Glamorgan (Lord's) 1934
7th 271* E. Hendren & F. T. Mann v. Nottinghamshire
(Nottingham) 1925
8th 182* M. H. C. Doll & H. R. Murrell v. Nottinghamshire (Lord's) 1913
9th 160* E. Hendren & T. J. Durston v. Essex (Leyton)... 1927
10th 230 R. W. Nicholls & W. Roche v. Kent (Lord's)...... 1899

NORTHAMPTONSHIRE

Highest Inngs. Totals: For ... 557–6d v. Sussex (Hove) 1914
Agst... 670–9d by Sussex (Hove)...... 1921
Lowest Inngs. Totals: For ... 12 v. Gloucestershire (Gloucester) 1907
Agst... 46 by Derbyshire (Northampton) 1912
Highest Indiv. Inngs.: For ... 300 R. Subba Row v. Surrey (Oval) 1958
Agst... 333 K. S. Duleepsinhji for Sussex (Hove) 1930
Most runs in a season 2198 (av. 51.11) D. Brookes 1952
runs in a career 28980 (av. 36.13) D. Brookes 1934–59
100s in a season 8 by R. Haywood 1921
100s in a career 67 by D. Brookes 1934–59
wkts. in a season 175 (av. 18.70) G. Tribe 1955
wkts. in a career 1097 (av. 21.31) E. W. Clark........ 1922–47

RECORD WICKET STANDS

1st	361	N. Oldfield & V. H. Broderick v. Scotland (Peterborough)	1953
2nd	307*	L. Livingston & D. Barrick v. Sussex (Northampton)	1953
3rd	320	L. Livingston & F. Jakeman v. South Africans (Northampton)	1951
4th	232	G. J. Thompson & S. G. Smith v. Hampshire (Portsmouth)	1910
5th	347	D. Brookes & D. Barrick v. Essex (Northampton)	1952
6th	376	R. Subba Row & A. Lightfoot v. Surrey (Oval)...	1958
7th	229	W. W. Timms & F. A. Walden v. Warwickshire (Northampton)	1926
8th	155	F. R. Brown & A. E. Nutter v. Glamorgan (Northampton)	1952
9th	156	R. Subba Row & S. Starkie v. Lancashire (Northampton)	1955
10th	148	B. Bellamy & V. Murdin v. Glamorgan (Northampton)	1925

NOTTINGHAMSHIRE

Highest Inngs. Totals: For ... 739–7d v. Leicestershire (Nottingham) 1903

Agst... 706–4d by Surrey (Nottingham) 1947

Lowest Inngs. Totals: For ... 13 v. Yorkshire (Nottingham) 1901

Agst... 16 (by Derbyshire and Surrey) ....1879 & 1880

Highest Indiv. Inngs.: For ... 312* W. W. Keeton v. Middlesex (Oval) 1939

Agst... 345 C. G. Macartney for Australians (Nottingham) 1921

Most runs in a season 2620 (av. 53.46) W. W. Whysall ... 1929

runs in a career 31327 (av. 36.71) G. Gunn 1902–32

100s in a season 9 by W. W. Whysall............... 1928

100s in a career 62 by J. Hardstaff 1930–55

wkts. in a season 181 (av. 14.96) B. Dooland 1954

wkts. in a career 1653 (av. 20.40) T. Wass 1896–1914

RECORD WICKET STANDS

1st	391	A. O. Jones & A. Shrewsbury v. Gloucestershire (Bristol)	1899
2nd	398	W. Gunn & A. Shrewsbury v. Sussex (Nottingham)	1890
3rd	369	J. Gunn & W. Gunn v. Leicestershire (Nottingham)	1903
4th	361	A. O. Jones & J. Gunn v. Essex (Leyton)	1905
5th	266	A. Shrewsbury & W. Gunn v. Sussex (Hove)	1884
6th	303*	H. Winrow & P. F. Harvey v. Derbyshire (Nottingham)..	1947
7th	201	R. H. Howitt & R. Bagguley v. Sussex (Nottingham)	1896
8th	220	G. F. H. Heane & R. Winrow v. Somerset (Nottingham)..	1933
9th	167	W. McIntyre & G. Wootton v. Kent (Nottingham)	1869
10th	152	E. Alletson & W. Riley v. Sussex (Hove)...........	1911

Highest Inngs. Totals: For ... 675–9d v. Hampshire (Bath)... 1924
Agst... 811 by Surrey (Oval)............ 1899
Lowest Inngs. Totals: For ... 25 v. Gloucestershire (Bristol) 1947
Agst... 22 by Gloucestershire (Bristol) 1920
Highest Indiv. Inngs.: For ... 310 H. Gimblett v. Sussex
(Eastbourne)................... 1948
Agst... 424 A. C. MacLaren for Lan-
cashire (Taunton) 1895
Most runs in a season 2761 (av. 56.82) W. E. Alley 1961
runs in a career 21108 (av. 37.09) H. Gimblett......... 1935–54
100s in a season 10 by W. E. Alley 1961
100s in a career 49 by H. Gimblett 1935–54
wkts. in a season 169 (av. 19.24) A. W. Wellard ... 1938
wkts. in a career 2153 (av. 18.10) J. C. White 1909–37

RECORD WICKET STANDS
1st 346 H. T. Hewett & L. C. H. Palairet v. Yorkshire
(Taunton) 1892
2nd 286 J. C. W. MacBryan & M. D. Lyon v. Derbyshire
(Buxton) 1924
3rd 300 G. G. Atkinson & P. B. Wight v. Glamorgan (Bath) 1960
4th 200 H. Gimblett & G. E. S. Woodhouse v. Middlesex
(Taunton) 1946
5th 235 J. C. White & C. C. Case v. Gloucestershire
(Taunton) 1927
6th 265 W. E. Alley & K. Palmer v. Northamptonshire
(Northampton) 1961
7th 240 S. M. J. Woods & V. T. Hill v. Kent (Taunton)... 1898
8th 143* E. F. Longrigg & C. J. P. Barnwell v. Gloucestershire (Bristol) 1938
9th 183 C. Greetham & H. W. Stephenson v. Leicestershire (Weston-super-Mare) 1963
10th 143 J. J. Bridges & H. Gibbs v. Surrey (Weston-super-
Mare) 1919

SURREY

Highest Inngs. Totals:	For ...	811 v. Somerset (Oval).........	1899
	Agst...	705–8d by Sussex (Hastings)...	1902
Lowest Inngs. Totals:	For ...	16 v. Nottinghamshire (Oval)	1880
	Agst...	15 by M.C.C. (Lord's).........	1839
Highest Indiv. Inngs.:	For ...	357* R. Abel v. Somerset (Oval)	1899
	Agst...	300* F. Watson for Lancashire (Manchester)	1928
Most runs in a season		3246 (av. 72.13) T. Hayward	1906
runs in a career		43703 (av. 49.77) J. B. Hobbs	1905–34
100s in a season		13 by T. Hayward (1906) and J. B. Hobbs	1925
100s in a career		144 by J. B. Hobbs	1905–34
wkts. in a season		250 (av. 14.06) T. Richardson......	1895
wkts. in a career		1775 (av. 17.91) T. Richardson ...1892–1905

RECORD WICKET STANDS

1st	428	J. B. Hobbs & A. Sandham v. Oxford U. (Oval)...	1926
2nd	371	J. B. Hobbs & E. G. Hayes v. Hampshire (Oval)	1909
3rd	353	A. Ducat & E. G. Hayes v. Hampshire (Southampton)	1919
4th	448	R. Abel & T. Hayward v. Yorkshire (Oval)	1899
5th	308	J. N. Crawford & F. C. Holland v. Somerset (Oval)	1908
6th	298	A. Sandham & H. S. Harrison v. Sussex (Oval)...	1913
7th	200	T. F. Shepherd & J. W. Hitch v. Kent (Blackheath)	1921
8th	204	T. Hayward & L. C. Braund v. Lancashire (Oval)	1898
9th	168	E. R. T. Holmes & E. W. Brookes v. Hampshire (Oval)	1936
10th	173	A. Ducat & A. Sandham v. Essex (Leyton).........	1921

Highest Inngs. Totals:	For ...	705–8d v. Surrey (Hastings)...	1902
	Agst...	726 by Nottinghamshire (Nottingham)	1895
Lowest Inngs. Totals:	For ...	19 v. Nottinghamshire (Hove)	1873
	Agst...	18 by Kent (Gravesend)......	1867
Highest Indiv. Inngs.:	For ...	333 K. S. Duleepsinhji v. Northants (Hove)	1930
	Agst...	322 E. Paynter for Lancashire (Hove)	1937
Most runs in a season		2850 (av. 64.77) John Langridge ...	1949
runs in a career		34152 (av. 37.69) John Langridge ...	1928–55
100s in a season		12 by John Langridge...............	1949
100s in a career		76 by John Langridge...............	1928–55
wkts. in a season		198 (av. 13.45) M. W. Tate.........	1925
wkts. in a career		2223 (av. 16.34) M. W. Tate.........	1912–37

RECORD WICKET STANDS

1st	490	E. H. Bowley & John Langridge v. Middlesex (Hove)	1933
2nd	385	E. H. Bowley & M. W. Tate v. Northamptonshire (Hove).....................................	1921
3rd	298	K. S. Ranjitsinhji & E. H. Killick v. Lancashire (Hove).....................................	1901
4th	326*	G. Cox & James Langridge v. Yorkshire (Leeds)	1949
5th	297	J. H. Parks & H. W. Parks v. Hampshire (Portsmouth)	1937
6th	255	K. S. Duleepsinhji & M. W. Tate v. Northamptonshire (Hove)	1930
7th	344	K. S. Ranjitsinhji & W. Newham v. Essex (Leyton)	1902
8th	229*	C. L. A. Smith & G. Brann v. Kent (Hove).........	1902
9th	178	H. W. Parks & A. F. Wensley v. Essex (Horsham)	1930
10th	156	G. R. Cox & H. R. Butt v. Cambridge U. (Cambridge)	1908

WARWICKSHIRE

Highest Inngs. Totals: For ... 657–6d v. Hampshire (Birmingham) 1899

Agst... 887 by Yorkshire (Birmingham) 1896

Lowest Inngs. Totals: For ... 16 v. Kent (Tonbridge) 1913

Agst... 15 by Hampshire (Birmingham) 1922

Highest Indiv. Inngs.: For ... 305* F. R. Foster v. Worcestershire (Dudley)......... 1914

Agst... 316 R. H. Moore for Hants. (Bournemouth)............... 1937

Most runs in a season   2417 (av. 60.42) M. J. K. Smith...... 1959

runs in a career   34172 (av. 35.31) W. G. Quaife ...1894–1928

100s in a season   8 by R. E. S. Wyatt 1937

100s in a career   71 by W. G. Quaife 1894–1928

wkts. in a season   180 (av. 15.13) W. E. Hollies 1946

wkts. in a career   2201 (av. 20.45) W. E. Hollies 1932–57

RECORD WICKET STANDS

1st 377* N. F. Horner & K. Ibadulla v. Surrey (Oval)...... 1960

2nd 344 J. Devey & S. P. Kinneir v. Derbyshire (Birmingham) 1900

3rd 327 S. P. Kinneir & W. G. Quaife v. Lancashire (Birmingham) 1901

4th 319 R. E. S. Wyatt & H. E. Dollery v. Lancashire (Birmingham)....................................... 1937

5th 268 W. Quaife & W. G. Quaife v. Essex (Leyton)...... 1900

6th 220 H. E. Dollery & J. Buckingham v. Derbyshire (Derby) 1938

7th 250 H. E. Dollery & J. S. Ord v. Kent (Maidstone)... 1953

8th 228 A. J. Croom & R. E. S. Wyatt v. Worcestershire (Dudley) 1925

9th 154 G. W. Stephens & A. J. Croom v. Derbyshire (Birmingham)....................................... 1925

10th 128 F. R. Santall & W. Sanders v. Yorkshire (Birmingham) 1930

Highest Inngs. Totals:	For ...	633 v. Warwickshire (Worcester)	1906
	Agst...	701–4d by Leicestershire (Worcester)	1906
Lowest Inngs. Totals:	For ...	24 v. Yorkshire (Huddersfield)	1903
	Agst...	30 by Hampshire (Worcester)	1903
Highest Indiv. Inngs.:	For ...	276 F. L. Bowley v. Hampshire (Dudley)	1914
	Agst...	331* J. D. Robertson for Middlesex (Worcester) ...	1949
Most runs in a season		2654 (av. 52.03) H. H. Gibbons ...	1934
runs in a career		30102 (av. 35.70) D. Kenyon	1946–63
100s in a season		9 by C. F. Walters	1933
100s in a career		64 by D. Kenyon......................	1946–63
wkts. in a season		207 (av. 17.52) C. F. Root	1925
wkts. in a career		2143 (av. 23.73) R. T. D. Perks ...	1930–55

RECORD WICKET STANDS

1st	309	F. L. Bowley & H. K. Foster v. Derbyshire (Derby)	1901
2nd	274	H. H. Gibbons & Nawab of Pataudi v. Kent (Worcester)..	1933
	274	H. H. Gibbons & Nawab of Pataudi v. Glamorgan (Worcester)..	1934
3rd	315	W. V. Fox & L. G. Crawley v. Northamptonshire (Worcester)..	1923
4th	277	H. H. Gibbons & B. W. Quaife v. Middlesex (Worcester)..	1931
5th	393	E. G. Arnold & W. B. Burns v. Warwickshire (Birmingham)..	1909
6th	195	G. N. Foster & J. A. Cuffe v. Leicestershire (Worcester)..	1913
7th	197	H. H. Gibbons & R. Howorth v. Surrey (Oval)...	1938
8th	145*	F. Chester & W. H. Taylor v. Essex (Worcester)...	1914
9th	181	J. A. Cuffe & R. O. Burrows v. Gloucestershire (Worcester)..	1907
10th	119	W. B. Burns & G. A. Wilson v. Somerset (Worcester)	1906

YORKSHIRE

Highest Inngs. Totals: For ... 887 v. Warwickshire (Birmingham) 1896
Agst... 630 by Somerset (Leeds) 1901
Lowest Inngs. Totals: For ... 26 v. Surrey (Oval)............ 1909
Agst... 13 by Nottinghamshire (Nottingham) 1901
Highest Indiv. Inngs.: For ... 341 G. H. Hirst v. Leicestershire (Leicester)...................... 1905
Agst... 318* W. G. Grace for Gloucestershire (Cheltenham)...... 1876
Most runs in a season   2883 (av. 80.08) H. Sutcliffe 1932
runs in a career   38561 (av. 50.21) H. Sutcliffe 1919–45
100s in a season   12 by H. Sutcliffe 1932
100s in a career   112 by H. Sutcliffe 1919–45
wkts. in a season   240 (av. 12.72) W. Rhodes 1900
wkts. in a career   3608 (av. 16.00) W. Rhodes.........1898–1930

RECORD WICKET STANDS

1st	555	P. Holmes & H. Sutcliffe v. Essex (Leyton).........	1932
2nd	346	W. Barber & M. Leyland v. Middlesex (Sheffield)	1932
3rd	323*	H. Sutcliffe & M. Leyland v. Glamorgan (Huddersfield)	1928
4th	312	G. H. Hirst & D. Denton v. Hampshire (Southampton)	1914
5th	340	E. Wainwright & G. H. Hirst v. Surrey (Oval)...	1899
6th	276	M. Leyland & E. Robinson v. Glamorgan (Swansea)	1926
7th	254	D. C. F. Burton & W. Rhodes v. Hampshire (Dewsbury)...	1919
8th	292	Lord Hawke & R. Peel v. Warwickshire (Birmingham)	1896
9th	192	G. H. Hirst & S. Haigh v. Surrey (Bradford)......	1898
10th	148	Lord Hawke & D. Hunter v. Kent (Sheffield)......	1898

"NEXT MAN IN"
Let's all try to help him.

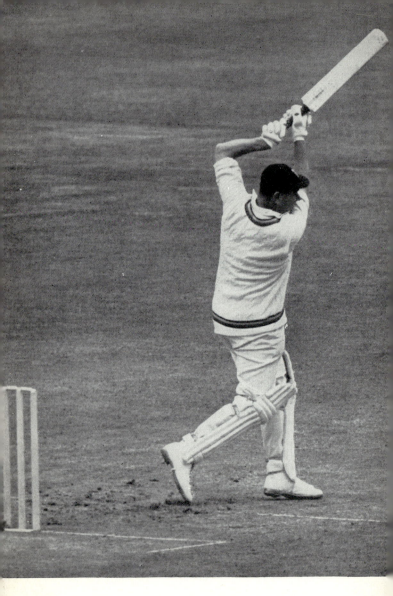

COLIN COWDREY

"No need to run" – The full face of the bat has been kept on the line in the
follow through.

DENIS COMPTON

"Four through the covers" – using every inch of his height for a forcing back
stroke. The keeper is right on the line with his balance inwards.

NEIL ADCOCK

"Resolute hostility." The head is looking at the target from behind the left arm: the action gives the feeling of control and power.

BRIAN STATHAM

"That's what gives it life." The "whipped" end of the long arc of his delivery swing.

DEREK SHACKLETON
"No day too long for him." A perfect follow through.

GARFIELD SOBERS

"That's beaten third man." The lash-like follow through of a full-bladed cut.

DAVID ALLEN

"Flight and spin." The left leg has not "buckled"; the arm has swept across
the body, and the wrist has pivoted to spin the ball.

ARTHUR McINTYRE

"Safe and sound." The hands have "ridden" with the ball.

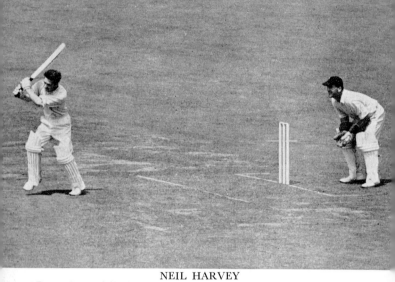

NEIL HARVEY
"Down the track." The batsman has used his feet to turn a flighted length ball into a half volley; the head and arms have led the balance into the drive.

TREVOR BAILEY
"Catches win matches." A half-chance magnificently taken.

A STAR OF TODAY, AND PERHAPS A STAR OF TOMORROW
George Eastham, formerly of Newcastle United and now Arsenal, chats with
a young admirer. There is nothing like meeting the stars to stimulate interest
in the young.

GYULA GROSICS

Hungary's famous goal-keeper in action. It is difficult to realize, looking at
the empty terraces, that this is a World Cup match in 1962 between Hungary
and England and Grosics has just saved a header by Johnny Haynes.

JACK KELSEY

A familiar sight on the football grounds of the world. Jack Kelsey, the Welsh goal-keeper is diving through the air to save a pile-driver.

THE MASTER'S GREATEST MOMENT
Stanley Matthews making the pass which won the 1953 Cup Final for Blackpool, after Bolton had looked almost certain winners.

JIMMY ARMFIELD TO THE RESCUE
Springett, England's goal-keeper is thankful to have Jimmy Armfield for a full-back against Switzerland at Wembley in 1962. This is a perfect example of a full-back's covering.

BILLY WRIGHT'S CENTURY

As he leads out an England team for his one hundredth cap. In all he played 105 times for England – a great record and a great sportsman.

STANLEY MATTHEWS

Is he the greatest footballer of all time? With his deceptive body swerve and
speed off the mark he has tormented many an experienced full-back.

JIMMY McILROY
A master of the deep-lying inside forward game who makes goals rather than scores them. A giant of a fine Burnley side, before being transferred to Stoke City.

ALFREDO DI STEFANO

"You must be able to do anything with a ball" is the advice this star of Real Madrid gives to young players. In this picture di Stefano goes through a juggling act to prove his complete mastery.

A DRAMATIC MOMENT

Johnny Haynes, on the ground, appears to have scored an equalizing goal for England against Scotland at Hampden Park in 1962, the shot first having hit the bar. The Dutch referee, however, said "No goal."

THE GOAL-KEEPER WENT THE WRONG WAY

Many goal-keepers, because of only a split second of time available to save a penalty, decide which way they are going before the kicker takes aim. In this case, Blacklaw of Burnley has guessed wrong in the 1962 Cup Final as Blanchflower scores for 'Spurs.

REAL MADRID
hoist the European Cup having just won it for the fifth successive year.

GREAT TEAMS

TOTTENHAM HOTSPUR
take the F.A. Cup back to a jubilant dressing-room at Wembley in 1961 the year they brought off the double.

FOOTBALL

THE CONTRIBUTORS –

Walter Winterbottom
Gyula Grosics
Jack Kelsey
Jimmy Armfield
Billy Wright
Stanley Matthews
Jimmy McIlroy
Alfredo di Stefano
Jack Clough

Some People Have Strange Notions About Coaching

by Walter Winterbottom

WHEREVER football is played there is usually plenty of argument about styles of play and methods of training. The success of a team seems to depend upon many closely related factors and it is impossible to say which is most important. Indeed, anyone who plays or watches football very soon forms his own convictions about matters of training, selection and tactics. There is every reason to believe that the game's popularity is partly because it provides many controversial issues to set people talking, and somehow there are always abundant examples of successful players and teams to prove one's point.

However, there are two essential requirements of a player which everyone accepts. To achieve the highest grades of performance, a player must first be gifted with skill and ability and then from a young age he must dedicate himself to practice. It is one of the functions of a coach, and a test of his qualities of leadership, to be able to encourage players of all ages to work hard to improve their skill. Enough evidence is available to show that well-directed training will achieve better results for the individual and the team. It is foolish to expect any system of training or coaching to make great players out of average material, but, nevertheless, players of ordinary ability will play better if they practise regularly and attempt to weld their individual styles and moves into good team work.

There will always be the few exceptionally gifted players whose skill and quickness of reaction make them outstanding. They require little personal coaching, but again they must practise with their team mates to create that instinctive understanding of each other's play. It is the job of a coach to plan the training of the team and to help to co-ordinate the special talents of each player. Some people have the strange notion that a coach tends to make all his players alike. Even if it were desirable to do so, it is really quite impossible to mould players to the same pattern. In pure physical skill each differs from the other, like fingerprints, and if you consider also the differences of temperament it is absurd to think of attempting to make one player like another.

In athletics and swimming, where it is possible to measure achievement accurately by time and distance, there has been remarkable progress over the last 50 years. Here are some figures which speak for themselves:

100 METRES

1924	Abrahams – 10.6 seconds (Olympic record)
1936	Owen – 10.3 seconds (Olympic record)
1960	Hary – 10.2 seconds (Olympic record)

1,500 METRES

1924	Nurmi – 3 mins. 53.6 secs. (Olympic record)
1936	Lovelock – 3 mins. 47.8 secs. (Olympic record)
1960	Elliott – 3 mins. 35.6 secs. (Olympic record)

HIGH JUMP

1924	Osborne – 6 ft. 6 ins. (Olympic record)
1936	Johnson – 6 ft. 8 ins. (Olympic record)
1960	Shav Lakadze and Brumel – 7 ft. 1 in. (Olympic record)

WEIGHT

1924	Hauser – 49 ft. 2¼ ins.
1936	Woelke – 53 ft. 1¾ ins. (Olympic record)
1960	Nieder – 64 ft. 6¾ ins. (Olympic record)

SWIMMING – 100 METRES FREE STYLE

1924	Weismuller – 59 secs.
1936	Szik – 57.6 secs.
1960	Devett – 55.2 secs.

SWIMMING – 400 METRES

1924	Weismuller – 5 mins. 4.2 secs.
1936	Medica – 4 mins. 44.5 secs.
1960	Rose – 4 mins. 18.3 secs.

Unfortunately there are no means of making similar comparisons in football, but we should not be blind to the fact that improvement has steadily taken place over the same period. We learn by experience and the coach must use the knowledge from past experience in order to improve performance of his players. New techniques, arising from constant experiments, are today helping footballers to reach higher peaks of fitness and attain greater skill. Some tests which have been made in Europe show the trained footballer to be in the highest bracket of stamina fitness when compared with men of other sports and games. The old fashioned method of lapping the field for stamina training has now given way to special running activities demanding all-out effort for short intervals, followed by a rest and then another effort and so on, until in a very short time the player is exhausted. This form of pressure training brings the footballer to a state of fitness related closely to the needs of the most gruelling game. The coach is essential to stimulate players in these new training routines.

However, it is in the realm of co-ordinated play where major changes have taken place and where the greatest scope for further improvement seems to lie. Occasionally, glimpses of very high speed interpassing and movement of rare accuracy and cunning leave the spectator spellbound. It is the task of top coaches the world over to co-ordinate individual skill to produce this exceptional type of play as demanded by the game situation. Much depends upon the attitude of the players and their willingness to persevere to reach higher performances. In the long run it is the players who by dint of competition and the effort of striving for better results, will raise standards. The good coach can assist by setting the right training atmosphere which stimulates and encourages the players.

Gyula Grosics, The Great Hungarian,

looks at goal-keeping the Continental way

This distinguished Hungarian goal-keeper will rank as one of the truly "Greats" in the game; certainly many English players who have played against him take this view. Grosics was in goal in the last World Cup when Hungary beat England. He has a shrewd brain and tactical approach to the game.

I STILL retain a vivid memory of the happenings at the World Cup in Chile. One of the most pleasant of these memories was in the match against the English eleven in which we were victorious once again after a great struggle. Soccer players are always filled with joy if their team can win against a side showing highly cultured play and boasting a glorious past. Our victory against England's soccer team has been very valuable for me because of all these considerations.

I was always pleased to be in a Hungarian team playing against the English national eleven or a club side. At these matches one could always count on real sportsmanship and highly exciting games. The goal-keepers of both sides had to keep their wits about them. It is a source of special pride for me never to have been in a Hungarian side which had lost to an English opponent.

In the past few years, in fact ever since I have been entertaining the idea of withdrawing from active sports life, I have spent a lot of time in studying the theoretical background of football. These years have deepened in me the feeling of appreciation towards English football. It was Moon of the Corinthians, Robinson, and many other world-famous English goal-keepers who had been the pioneers of this art and they showed the way for all Europe's goal-keepers. The fact that the Hungarians were good pupils has been amply proved by them and can be measured in the achievements of their goalies. Let me just mention the names of Ferenc Zsák and Ferenc Plattkó from among my excellent predecessors who have not only mastered the motion style of English goalies but had developed it to some extent.

Recently I have started writing a book about my sports career. In the course of my work I have given an account of my experiences in the development of goal-keeping technique. I have found it singular that although the sporting press had considered my style as revolutionarily new, there had been a fairly high number of goal-keepers in the past who had shown similar merits, duly recorded.

When I think of my successes in goal, it always occurs to me how much I owe to the Hungarian coaches who had perfected my style from early adolescence. They were always teaching me the features they had considered very good in the style and play of my predecessors – and I imbibed their teaching like dry earth absorbs rain water.

I am often confused these days when engaged on the basic training of young goal-keepers because I can no longer remember which of the training methods are due to my old coaches and which are the upshots of my own experience. I feel that this is as it should be. The country which wishes to have high football standards has to respect and utilize the experiences of the predecessors and the present-day *élite*.

I have come to the end of the journey. It is in the order of things that pupils later become teachers themselves. I take my profession seriously and so I should like my pupils to outdo me ultimately on the football ground and to develop the existing techniques to a higher degree.

Hungary's football history shows many examples of international goal-keepers turning into football leaders who influence the trend of developments in Hungary's football life. Such was, among others, Ödön Hollits who wrote a book with Dr. Mihàly Mamusich on football, based on English experiences which had determined the trend of Hungary's football development for dozens of years. Also, Tibor Gallovich, the one-time outstanding goal-keeper, ultimately became Hungary's team manager. I myself am deeply indebted to him for what he had done to make me a 'keeper of the national eleven's goal.

GENERAL OUTLINES

Speaking about goal-keeping in general, I think that the training of future goal-keepers should be started at an early age. The early training methods are yet to be evolved because the present ones are mainly just general outlines. It is no immodesty on my part if I now refer to my own case. At Dorog, which is my native town, I had spent most of my time on the football ground as early as nine, while by the age of fourteen I was moving around so skilfully that they put me into the senior team. From that moment my regular training under a proper coach's control was assured.

A prime mover of my development has been my industry springing from my love of football. I felt so strongly about this that I gave myself no liberties and would not suffer any setback. In this way I ensured constant development. The confidence which I had felt towards my coaches had also acted as an impetus. Little wonder therefore that I had always concentrated hard during training bouts.

In analysing the physical characteristics of goal-keepers it must be mentioned that any interference by the goal-keeper in the field play, the tackling of a shot, or the act of hurling oneself at the attacker's feet to nip the ball off them, require a maximum burst of effort of one or two seconds at most. I can bear out this statement by saying that in a well-kicked penalty shot the ball doesn't take more than 0.05 second to travel from the penalty point to the goal. And the goal-keepers who have quick reflexes and an instinctive feeling for making the right move will frequently do the impossible and save the penalty kick.

For short bursts of energy the whole of the so-called absolute muscular strength must be summoned but the system must be accustomed to lasting efforts as well. We can only attain this by suitable training.

BASIC REQUIREMENT

For a goal-keeper's effective play the basic requirement is the natural aptitude, of course, but he must also reach a state of trained preparedness which permits him short maximum bursts of energy and prompt reflexes even during a prolonged period of strain.

This is how the major physical properties, such as strength, stamina, speed and skilfulness develop fully to make high performances possible in the player. Simultaneously with these, mental capacities gradually emerge in the course of training and play their role in the decisions and actions side by side with the physical attributes.

In tackling balls sharply shot towards the corners by

diving for them, mental capacities determine the co-ordination of the movements while physical capacities manifest themselves in resilience and ball sense.

Among the capacities, special importance attaches to general skilfulness which must be developed in goal-keepers with the greatest care, beginning at the early age.

I consider the sense of skilful movement very important because it provides the major background of the goal-keeper's special skills. Just think how unskilful a young child can be when he has to catch a ball thrown towards him. He would drop the ball because he still lacks the feeling for the correct movement. Later on, with the development of this feeling, his skilfulness will increase. This then is the time when the development of ball-game players, including soccer players, should begin.

In the first period of acquiring the feeling for the correct movement, we still find much superfluous effort and un-necessary secondary movements. However, after a suitable length of training time, the movements became more con-scious and to the purpose.

MECHANICAL PERFORMANCE

In studying the correct movements, the major requirement is a concentration of one's attention on performance. To wit, the mechanical performance of movements excludes con-scious action and may lead to faulty reflexes.

In the near future, a special regular goal-keepers' course will be started at the sports training camp at Tata, West Hungary. At this course, the regular training of goal-keepers will begin under my direction. The best Hungarian goal-keepers will enter this course, side by side with young up-and-coming goalies to whom special attention will be paid.

At our goal-keepers' course, we shall try to provide efficient training based on scientific findings and make up for the absence at present of a suitable number of occasional foot-ball grounds for youth. A goal-keepers' course of this nature should ensure quick and efficient progress.

We are planning to provide accommodation at the sports training camp at Tata for some foreign students too. I should be delighted to be able to coach one or another of the gifted English goal-keepers at our course.

Among the goal-keeper's many necessary skills, leaps and bounds are very important. In saving high and low shots alike, the goal-keeper has to perform his leaps with precision. Major conditions of a well-performed leap make up a long list: resilience, strength, sense of rhythm, space and balance, harmony in movement, skilfulness, courage, attention and speed. And in modern football all these capacities and attributes must be developed by application.

In the foregoing I have tried to outline a few thoughts about the technicalities which have to be taken into consideration in training the future goal-keeper generation to bring goal-keeping to a more up-to-date level.

TRAINING BOUTS

The tests of a goal-keeper's skills are his performances week by week during the actual matches. Based on the observations made at these matches, the agenda for the training bouts can be drawn up. During my career, it was at the building-up bout following each match that we evaluated the lessons drawn from the match. I have always paid great attention at such bouts to practise certain features in order to eliminate faulty moves I had shown at previous matches. Remembering single incidents helps a lot because if a goal-keeper blatantly fails to save a weak shot he will visualize the faulty move in his mind for many days to come and sometimes even for years.

In my individual training methods an important role was always given over to practising dives. I have paid special attention to getting used to ground dives so as to master the instinctive revulsion before expected pain. For this one needs courage and a lot of will-power. We can say that in the course of the goal-keeper's training the practising of mid-air and ground dives is of the essence. I consider it very useful for a goal-keeper to practise with two or three balls while lying on the ground. The vigorousness of turning round while lying greatly promotes the development of swift reflexes in jumping up from the ground and tackling short-range shots.

Practising the efficient stopping or catching of the ball is a permanent feature of the goal-keeper's training. Special attention must be paid to develop the necessary reflexes to make the ball "stick" in the goal-keeper's hands. I have practised this a lot myself with rebounds from either the posts or from any suitable wall.

I feel that I must speak at some length about running out of the goal to meet an oncoming attacker or, in other words, playing the role of a fourth back. In my view, the capacity for correct timing requires a natural aptitude which is given in all players to a smaller or greater extent. However, this also means that the aptitude cannot be mastered by practising only but the given aptitude can be greatly developed by training.

EFFICIENT TEAMWORK

Harmony between the full-backs and the goal-keeper is of the greatest importance. A basic condition of efficient teamwork between the four players is the thorough knowledge of each other's style of play. For this purpose, there must be frequent talks between the goal-keepers and the full-backs at which the reasons for a successful or unsuccessful sortie from the goal can be analysed and suitable preparations made for adapting themselves to the style of play of the next opponent's forward line. As a result of such talks, a style of play can be developed whereby a full-back can judge merely by the position of the ball whether the goal-keeper will leave the goal for handling or kicking the ball or not. At a time like this, a full-back under normal circumstances tries to slow down the running opponent player's tempo. The other full-back would keep a lookout for a possible rebound which he can then kick back into the field.

It is a frequent mistake for goal-keepers to start out of the goal and then change their minds and stop half-way. Such hesitation gives the forward the necessary time for assessing his chance and acting. However, if the goal-keeper runs out to meet the attacker without stopping, he can embarrass him even if his timing is bad. But the most dangerous situation of all is for a goal-keeper to start backing after having left his goal.

Well, when should the goal-keeper rush out of his goal? That always depends on the situation at a given moment. The realization of the chances and odds in a given situation requires adequate football sense, experience, close attention, speed and resolution. It often occurs that the goal-keeper even runs out of the penalty box and kicks the ball far afield to relieve his goal of possible pressure. But he should only do this if there is no other choice because such a move on his part always entails risks.

In a well-timed sortie from the goal, a sense of position plays an important role. In the course of all the matches I ever played, I only stood actually on the goal line on the rarest of occasions, when the opponent's line of attack literally pinned me to the goal.

Towards the end of his sortie from the goal, the goal-keeper often has to dive for the ball. I have only hurled myself before the feet of an attacker if there was absolutely no other solution. In such cases I have always tried to shut off the angle of approach before the attacker and execute my dive in the simplest and quickest possible way. I have always tried to "glide" into the line of shooting so as to avoid the possibility of the ball slipping across under me.

I should like to stress that a sortie can only be successful if the goal-keeper follows the whole of the game with the closest attention and does not relent for a single moment. He should follow the course of the ball even if the game swings over to the opponents' half of the ground and as soon as the ball returns over the half line, he must stand ready to interfere at any emergency.

The goal-keeper must have a lot of training as a field player, too, in order to be able to fill the role of a fourth back. At training matches for two goals, there are no risks so he can leave the goal line at wish.

Elderly football fans still remember the old saying "a corner is almost sure to produce a goal". Well, this saying is becoming obsolescent because experience shows that nowadays very few goals are scored as a result of corner shots. In my judgement, a sufficiently tall, resilient and efficient goal-keeper should be able to pull down or hit out a high centre pass descending between the penalty point and the goal. Of course, his own team's field players have also got to fill certain roles during corner shots. It is important that one or two players should cover the unmanned goal and the best header among the defence players should mark the opponent's best header.

The goalkeeper's role is basically different from that of the field players and so he requires specific training methods to ensure adequate form. Throughout my career, I have considered it very important to do regular gymnastic exercises, including acrobatic features, and undergo simultaneous athletic training. At my training bouts, the fans could always see me practising high jump, and exercises with the skipping rope and medicine ball. These have all proved extremely useful.

The "science of football" now fills the paper of many reference works. Accordingly, it is no easy matter to give a full picture about goal-keeping in such a short article. However, I do hope that some of the things which I have said here have evoked certain thoughts which might be useful for my English goal-keeper friends.

Jack Kelsey, of Wales,

Britain's most capped goal-keeper, talks about the British way

Rated as the best goal-keeper in Great Britain, Jack Kelsey had won over 40 International caps for Wales before injury distressingly put him out of the game just before the start of the 1962–63 season. Becoming an Arsenal professional in 1949 Kelsey has made 327 appearances for his club in League football – a remarkable record.

WHEN someone asked me one day what I thought were the main problems a goal-keeper has to face I sat down for a moment or two and jotted them down on a piece of paper. I still have that piece of paper upon which is written – "Peak fitness; the appreciation of angles; changing conditions; calling; corner kicks; penalties; defensive walls; use of the ball; ground shots; through balls".

Lumped together like that it all sounds rather bewildering and might give the impression that you need to go to a University to learn all about it, but I hope you will have changed your mind when I say a few words about each heading, and I can prove to you that goal-keeping is very much a worthwhile job if you take it seriously and are ready to learn all the time.

Remembering that goal-keeping is a specialist position, the training for it is also specialist. The ordinary player does plenty of running in his training to build up stamina; the goal-keeper is primarily concerned with agility and with this in mind trunk bending from the waist plays an important part. This is invaluable training for a situation in a match which is always cropping up when after moving for a shot the ball is deflected and a sudden change of direction is necessary. Playing fast ball games like tennis, table tennis and squash can work wonders for agility and reflexes. In addition it is imperative for a goal-keeper to be quick off the mark when he is required to dash out to the edge of the penalty area; for this short bursts of running about twenty-five yards should form part of the training.

A VITAL WORD

Angles . . . what a vital word in goal-keeping techniques.

Narrow the angle and expose as little of the goal as possible when a forward is about to shoot. Just think about this one for a moment. If a forward is about to shoot from the edge of the penalty area and the goal-keeper stands in the middle of his goal and on the goal line, it means that he has four yards to cover between himself and each upright. The chances are that if it is a well-placed shot just inside an upright he will fail to reach it. If, on the other hand, he moves forward about four yards, he has now cut down the target area to about two yards either side of him. But always remember . . . don't come too far out because the pace of the shot will beat you.

Try this experiment that I used to use in my very early days in the game for which a wooden stake and about fifty yards of string is necessary. Take one end of the string and tie it to an upright. Place the stake in the ground at any point on the edge of the penalty area, pass the string round the stake and tie the loose end to the other upright. The string, then, represents the two uprights, and if the goal-keeper takes up a position on the goal line between the two lines of string and then moves forward towards the stake, he will soon find the most suitable angle where he will be in a position to deal with any shot that comes within the string lines. An important point about moving out of goal towards an advancing forward is that the man with the ball, noticing the goal-keeper advancing, may well try to lob the ball over his head. Always expect this to happen, a slow high lob might give you the chance to move backwards and catch the ball. If it catches you unawares you might have to go into one of those back-breaking leaps to turn the ball over the bar. Experience will develop a natural habit of finding the right spot to cover every angle.

EVERY CONDITION

You have heard, of course, in racing circles of how one particular horse likes the going soft, whereas another prefers it hard. A football goal-keeper has to perform at his best in every condition, and playing in the winter months in England certainly gives you plenty of variety. You can play on successive days and have totally different conditions. On a bone-hard surface it pays to be first to the ball without waiting for it to bounce, especially when under pressure. Good positioning on hard grounds is absolutely essential because it saves you diving about all over the place and taking some hard knocks. In the real winter the wet and greasy ball is the goal-keeper's bugbear. I believe that string gloves are essential for getting a better grip, but even with gloves the ball can be as slippery as an eel. It is always better in certain situations in wet weather to punch the ball away rather than try to grasp it. You will also find that low shots tend to pick up speed after hitting the slippery ground so you must have your whole body behind the ball in case it goes through your hands. The body is then a second line of defence.

A goal-keeper must be equipped with a good pair of hands, a good pair of feet, and also, a good voice! A goal-keeper is so placed that he can see the whole of the field and he must never shirk the responsibility of giving a colleague a warning call. Take the case of a defender facing his own goal with the ball at his feet and believing that he is free to turn and pass the ball away. Without eyes in the back of his head he cannot see an opponent about to tackle him. If he should lose the ball in these circumstances it is the goal-keeper's fault unless he has shouted a warning.

An analysis will show that very few goals are scored from corner kicks these days. This is not because the forwards have forgotten how to shoot, but because the modern defensive plan is too efficient, and in this, the goal-keeper plays a principal role. He has two ways of clearing – catching or punching. The goal-keeper normally takes up a position at the upright farthest away from where the corner is being taken. He faces the kicker, and from this position he can see at a glance all that is going on. He takes command of the six-yard area and any ball coming across or dropping in this area is his. If he feels that his path is clear to move out to take it without the possibility of being obstructed, he should let his colleagues know of his intentions by shouting "My Ball" and then make every effort to catch it.

WORD OF WARNING

Supposing now, another situation, where the goal-keeper is likely to be challenged from behind by the opposite winger who is moving in fast. The goal-keeper, eye on the ball, doesn't see him coming. This time a word of warning from his full-backs, who would be positioned at each upright, such as "Watch your back" would let him know of the challenge. In these circumstances it would be unwise to try and catch the ball, so he can either punch it upfield, or flick it across the goal-mouth into the empty space the on-coming winger has created. The full-back sensing this might happen is ready to go out and collect the loose ball. The punch would also be used if the ball is anywhere near the cross-bar or just under. If an opponent is on the spot, push it over the bar. Inswinging corners should also be tipped over; outswingers should be left to the defenders, especially if the ball is swinging away outside the six-yard line.

Now what about penalties – the goal-keeper's nightmare. Some goal-keepers say they are not a nightmare because you are not expected to save them, anyway. I say you are on the field to try and save everything and whoever the taker may be, I never say to myself, "This is in the net" as he moves up to take the kick. Types of penalty shots are divided into two classes. The hard power shot aimed at breaking the back of the net, or the cleverly placed shot with perhaps a disguised run-up meant to lure the goal-keeper in the wrong direction. I always make a mental note of players who take their teams' penalties. If a player beats me with a kick to my left, he may well try to put subsequent kicks in the same place. I would then move that way next time. Most goal-keepers, I think, decide which way they are going before the kick is taken so they at least have a fifty per cent chance of going the right way.

HUMAN WALL

With a free-kick, the goal-keeper is not out on his own; he has his defenders to help him. Normally three players are linked together to form a wall. The end player in the wall lines himself up in a direct line between the near post and the ball, and ten yards in front of the ball. The other two players link arms with him to form a human wall which covers over half the goal-mouth. The remaining area is covered by the goal-keeper, but it is not as easy as it might seem. The goal-keeper has to be ready to move behind the wall if the free-kick is chipped over it, or to move forward if the kick is pushed to the inside of the wall for a second forward to run on and hit the ball. The goal-keeper has to be a jump ahead of every eventuality.

It might sound silly to suggest that a goal-keeper's function is to score goals as well as save them, but in an indirect way it is perfectly true. Very often today the goal-keeper is instrumental in setting up an attack by a well-placed kick or throw to a colleague. The aimless boot up field is dead and gone, because there is more than a fair chance that it will be collected by an opponent and all you have done is put them back on the attack. Supposing, for instance, a goal-keeper has just beaten off an opponents' attack down his right flank. Play, being over that side, means that the majority of their players through linking up will be over there and as a result they may be momentarily weak on the other side. A goal-keeper can exploit this temporary weakness with a well-aimed throw. A sudden change of flanks has always been a useful weapon.

Have you ever seen a really great goal-keeper beaten by a soft shot? Of course you have, it does happen, but it is usually brought about by a bad bounce or alternatively by a spinning ball. Remember this. The only way to deal with a ground shot is to get down on one knee with the body well behind the path of the ball. If you simply bend from the waist in an effort to pick the ball up, you are offering only the width of your legs as an emergency line of defence. A bad break of the ball can often go either side and a soft goal is scored, and there is nothing like a goal-keeper giving away a simple goal to upset the balance of a team. There is every possibility that each time a goal-keeper makes a mistake, the result is a goal. A centre-forward can make ten mistakes in a match and still score two winning goals.

WORST MOMENT

What is the worst moment in a goal-keeper's life – probably when an opposing forward is bearing down on him with a clear path to goal, having just picked up a through ball. This is where timing and courage come in. Usually the forward pushes the ball a yard or two in front of him – that is your time to pounce. On another occasion it might be advisable to advance beyond the penalty area if you think that the speed of the ball is such that it will not reach the area before the forward catches up with it. Never be afraid of coming out of the penalty area and booting the ball; never try and be clever and beat the forward by dribbling; that is something he can do better than you can. Can you imagine how silly you would look having lost the ball yards out of your goal?

The golden rule – "Eye always on the ball". Sometimes during the excitement of play a 'keeper can become lost positionally. This will mean that he will have to make a backward glance to one of the uprights so as to re-adjust his position in relation to them. In doing this he must take his eye off the ball for a split second – and a goal can be scored in that time. I have always made a mark on the six-yard line in the centre of the goal-mouth. It is so much easier to look down in front of me than to look behind to adjust my position.

Now to the last word. Practice . . . you can never have too much. I hope something I have said will help you save one of those near-certain goals some time. Good luck with your goal-keeping anyway. It has been the means of me seeing the world and making countless friends.

England Player, Jimmy Armfield,

reveals the secrets of being a good full-back

Jimmy Armfield has captained England. Came to the notice of the Blackpool Club while playing for Blackpool schoolboys. Soon made his name with his speed off the mark and intelligent positioning. Gained recognition with the Under 23 side before being capped in the full England eleven. Is now an automatic choice for his country.

COMPARED with, say, a forward or a goal-keeper, a full-back has a somewhat unspectacular job, but it is none the less an important one. I think I am in a fair position to judge because I started my career with Blackpool as an outside-right and only moved to full-back as a result of an accident. During a third team game one of our defenders was hurt and I was switched to full-back. This temporary move became a permanent one and now, looking back on the years that have followed, I appreciate more than ever the full and valuable part which a full-back plays in a team. I also contend that modern football enables a full-back to be more enterprising and perhaps bolder than his predecessors.

First, however, he must concentrate on becoming efficient in his primary role as guardian of his goal. He must never forget that he is the last but one barrier to his own goal and that he is there chiefly to prevent the other side scoring.

With this in mind he must carry out two essentials:

(1) Maintain a constant watch on the opposing attack, especially on the wing forward.

(2) Be on hand to give his centre-half full cover.

He cannot succeed in either unless he has sound positional sense. All too often, particularly in junior matches, a full-back clears the ball out of his sector of the field and then shows little interest in what happens afterwards.

ANY EMERGENCY

But a full-back who knows his job follows the game constantly and thoroughly, trying never to lose sight of the ball and to anticipate his opponent's next move so that he can position himself to deal with any emergency.

One spot a full-back dislikes being forced into is when he

faces two opponents – the centre-forward, with the ball, and, say, the outside-left. What should he do? I know what I do and to my way of thinking it is the logical solution to a tough problem.

I challenge the centre-forward and if I don't dispossess him at least I nearly always force him to pass to the winger away from the centre. Then I cut across to challenge the outside-left. It may seem like chasing around in circles but really I am employing delaying tactics while my colleagues in defence cover up.

Sometimes I am asked by young full-backs what is the best position for a full-back to take up for corners. Some full-backs stand practically on the goal line. I prefer to station myself one yard out from the near post (that is if the outside-left is taking the flag kick). In this way I do not impede the goal-keeper and I am in a handy position to move out to intercept the centre or to retreat back into goal if the centre curves in.

When the corner is taken on the opposite wing I position myself one yard *past* the far post. Again I am not interfering with my goal-keeper and yet I have complete freedom of movement. There is no goalpost blocking the way if the centre soars over my head. The full-back who does not have a full understanding with his centre-half and the other full-back puts his defence in a vulnerable position.

It is essential he offers maximum cover to the centre-half. For if the centre-half is pulled out of position, or loses possession, and nobody is covering up the way to goal is wide open. Supposing a raid was being built down our left flank. I would then take up station in a diagonal line with the centre-half and the left-back.

WELL PLACED

I am thus able to move into the middle if the centre-half is pulled out yet I am also well placed to move back quickly into my own position if the opposing side suddenly switch the ball to their right wing.

Forwards are repeatedly switching the ball about these days and this is something a full-back should always be alive to.

Tackling, too, is a key part of a full-back's game. The defender who continually backs away or goes into the tackle half-heartedly will nearly always be beaten. Strength and determination must be put into the tackle – and always play the ball and not the man because the chances are that a misplaced tackle could cost a penalty.

Sometimes, of course, it is not possible, or wise, to make a tackle when the opposing winger is in possession. The only alternative is to try to jockey him towards the touchline. Don't let him burst through on the inside because then he could be presented with a clear path to goal.

NOT ONLY DEFENCE

But, as I said at the beginning, a full-back should not be satisfied with playing a purely defensive game. He should be eagerly on the look-out for the chance of mobilizing his own forwards.

Come out of defence with the ball quickly and, whenever possible, try to part with it intelligently. One move that can be effective is to co-operate with the wing-half in taking the ball upfield by a series of inter-passes. It is known as the "wall pass" and if operated slickly it can throw the opposition into confusion.

There are occasions, too, when a full-back finds the way open for him to advance with the ball well into his opponent's half. This is an advantage he should not let slip. He should get going – and keep going – and if the chance of a shot presents itself then he should take it.

But whatever the outcome of this sole move he should not stand still admiring his handiwork. He should get back into position *immediately*.

Speed off the mark. That is so essential to a full-back in these days of nippy wingers, inter-changing forwards and fast retreating defences. So build up speed off the mark and to do so practice 20-yard bursts.

To sum up:

Develop sound positional sense.

Maintain a close understanding with the centre-half and the other full-back.

Be nippy off the mark.

Be strong and determined in the tackle.

Be alert to the opportunity to change defence into attack.

Billy Wright,

105 times capped for England says, "Give me a strong half-back line"

Over a century of caps for England (105) and now Manager of Arsenal, Billy Wright has had a glittering football career. He spent all his playing days with one club – the famous Wolves, whom he joined at the age of fifteen. He led their Cup Winning team in the 1948–49 Season and the League Championship side in 1953–54.

"GIVE me a strong half-back line and I am happy." I have heard many a Manager say this, and although football is a game of eleven players each with an integral part to play of considerable importance, history tells us that the great sides were often made great by having a commanding set of half-backs. The half-back, is, after all, a double link. He is an attacking link with his forwards, and a defensive link with his backs. He is the pivot on which the side rotates; he can make goals . . . and give them away!

The three half-backs are essentially a unit and as such it is hardly fair to single one out as being more important than the other except that since the shortest route to goal is through the middle of the field the centre-half does assume that little extra bit of responsibility. A centre-half's slip has more chance of giving a goal away than a mistake by either wing-half, although they can be equally to blame. Remember, that every goal scored is somebody's mistake.

Yet whatever your position on the field the ultimate answer to it all is just the same . . . be a master of your skills . . . overcome the ball just as a racing car driver of great experience has complete control of his car and is thus better equipped to deal with a sudden situation which needs quick thinking and application. If you have been taught the basic elements of the game, and are fairly proficient in them, the next important step is how to apply them under match conditions. You might have decided in practice that you head the ball quite well . . . but where do you head it to? In a match when you are under pressure this is very important. It's no good being in the correct position to head the ball, and meeting it just right, if you send it straight to an opponent. So when you are practising, try and create match conditions. Get someone to kick the ball in the air to you when another player is challenging you for possession, with two other players standing by, one a colleague and one an opponent. You must head the ball to the colleague. Similarly, if you are a wing-half practising your throw-ins, don't just throw the ball vaguely into space; make up some team mates and opponents. Many of the things that we do so well when we have plenty of time we make a hash of when under pressure in a match. Often the skill factor goes altogether, particularly with boys.

But perhaps I am putting the cart before the horse. I believe that before you even start playing this game you should be prepared to completely dedicate yourself to it. Think football and dream football. Be prepared to play for ninety minutes in a match and keep going until the final whistle, whatever the score. Remember that every Manager has respect for a "Trier", and a big heart and determination can often make up for a lack of skill. If you have got both then so much the better and you'll probably get to the top of the tree.

The centre-half's job is to look after the centre-forward. Watch him and never let him out of your sight. He is going to try and draw you out of position; always be wary of this. More goals are scored by the centre-half being hopelessly drawn out of position when there was no need for him to go at all than in any other way. If the centre-forward is coming at you in possession of the ball get in quickly and tackle hard. Don't let him take you with him on some wanderings if where he is going he can be no danger to the play in progress. A team is most vulnerable through the middle and it is your job to block the middle; only leave it when you have a good reason and are fairly certain of getting the ball.

The wing-half, too, has to think about marking his man – in his case the inside-forward; mark him close and tackle hard, too. Always remember that you are still very much in the game even when you are not in possession of the ball. It is important that when the ball does come your way you are ready to receive it. If the ball is the other side of the field you still have to mark the inside-forward, you have still got to give the centre-half cover, as well as the full-back. I believe that the wing-half has an attacking role to play as well as a defensive one and I would always advocate a wing-half taking the ball through towards the opponents' goal if he sees an opening that he can exploit . . . and only if he does. I have no time for a wing-half who suddenly thinks that it would be nice to score a goal and marches upfield with no chance of creating an advantage. If a half-back sees his chance, and goes through, the man whose position he is taking drops back to cover. In other words if you are inside-left and you see your left-half coming through, drop back to cover the gap he has left . . . and wing-half . . . if you go up and lose the ball, don't stand with your hands on your hips and look towards Heaven as if it is somebody's fault up there that you have lost the ball . . . Get back as fast as you can to the position you have left. Make a point of going to first-class matches and spend the whole afternoon watching the player in your position. See where he is and what he is doing for all the ninety minutes. Then you will see what I mean by being in the game when you have not got possession of the ball.

If you have laid a long pass to the centre-forward don't regard that as your job done. Get into a good position in case he wants to give it back to you.

When your team is not in possession of the ball always make sure that you are goal-side of the man. When you are not in possession you must always be thinking how you are going to get possession, where you are going to get it, and how you are going to use the ball when you have got it. If you are ever faced with the sight of two players coming at you, one with the ball . . . NEVER TACKLE . . . because you are on a hiding to nothing . . . just retreat until some help comes from somewhere.

If you are taking a throw-in, bear in mind that you are a free man, so having thrown the ball in be ready to receive it back again. In other words, what I am trying to say is that you are thinking every minute you are on the field. You can certainly try out all sorts of dodges in practice; sometimes they will come off in a match, but often plans made before-hand go all wrong because there happens always to be another team on the field as well as your own and you will have to size up what they are doing and quickly work out something to counter them. It would be no good for instance feeding the centre-forward with high balls through the air if the opposing centre-half is 6 ft. 3 ins. There is always a chance that such a tall fellow might be a little slow on the turn and you would try and exploit that weakness if you find that it does exist.

If you have got a few tricks and like to show them off

occasionally, all well and good, provided you never choose your own penalty area to try them out. A ball in your own penalty area must not be allowed to stay there a moment longer than is necessary, and never be ashamed to push it back to your goal-keeper; that is often the safest way of clearing, but do make sure that he can see that it is coming. There is nothing more ridiculous than seeing a defender put the ball into his own net, or putting it in such a position that an attacker can move in and intercept the ball before the goal-keeper can get there. Yes, this does happen in top-class football, but the Manager usually has quite a few words to say about it in the dressing-room at half-time or after the match. It is hard enough to win matches without giving goals away and there is nothing more undermining to an attack which has perhaps scored a couple of good goals that have been hard-worked for, to see their efforts frittered away by slip-shod carelessness on the part of the defence.

Modern football with its intricate system of covering has created a defensive bloc; everybody on the field is a defender and everybody is an attacker. How often have decisive moves these days been initiated by a goal-keeper with a neat throw to one of his colleagues. Football is a team game. There is no room in it for a selfish player. If you pull your weight and earn the respect of your colleagues then I am sure that many happy hours of football lie ahead of you. I hope they will be as happy as my playing days which have provided me with a lifetime of friends and memories.

The Winger is Coming Into His Own

by Stanley Matthews

What can be said of the maestro that has not been said before?
The wizard of football, who will become a legend, first played
for Stoke City in the 1931–32 season, was transferred to
Blackpool in 1947 and then back to Stoke. Matthews made
his International debut against Wales in September, 1934, and
made 54 appearances, the last in the qualifying rounds of
the World Cup in 1957.

THE unparalleled success of foreign teams in world-class
football is rapidly changing the face of the game in this
country. New playing ideas and team policies – which have
brought with them fantastic triumphs – have forced our own
team bosses to reorganize their plans.

Look how the role of the centre-forward has changed. No
longer is he the human battering ram, the super-charged
force which crashed through to goal. Now he plays a more
subtle part in the game.

The fabulous Magyars from Hungary invented the deep-
lying leader. And immediately the move spread panic among
opposing defences. They could, apparently, find no answer
to this devastating plan of a will o' the wisp who popped up
in the most unexpected places.

In came, too, the square defence and the goal-blocking by
a full-scale retreat when opponents mounted attacks. Inside-
forwards, like Puskas, became the crack-shots – and they
were often schooled to be first-time marksmen.

CHANGING WORLD

In all this changing world of Soccer, the extreme winger
is finding that he, too, must play a different role. He is
becoming more and more the striker of the attack.

If you want two first-class examples, take those aces of the
wing – Garrincha (Brazil) and Gento, of Real Madrid. Here
you have terrifically fast wingers who are wonderfully skilful
in ball manipulation. And both of them have dynamite in
their boots.

So, here in England, the winger is coming into his own as
a match-winner. No longer does he split the defences and
make the goals – he scores them. All our top teams can lay

their success to the fantastic speed and quick-fire shooting of the wingers. Look at the scoring lists and you will get my meaning.

Men like Cliff Jones (Tottenham), Billy Bingham (Everton), John Connelly (Burnley), and Bobby Charlton (Manchester United) have all played a prominent part in their team victories. Their forceful and dynamic play are increasingly creating problems for the men who oppose them.

So now the match-winning winger is the ace for which all club managers are seeking. And lucky is the manager who can put two of them into his attack.

By all this I do not mean that the old role of the winger has gone. He still has a paramount task in drawing the attack away from the middle of the field. He must still have that perfect understanding with his colleagues alongside and behind him. And he must still have perfect control of the ball.

It is just an added foil to his armoury of attack. He no longer runs to the line and lobs the ball into the middle. He must be ready to cut in to goal and wait, like a hungry tiger, ready to pounce.

TOP SPEED

So the winger should be among the fastest men in a team. Their success depends on all moves being carried out at top speed. But we don't expect them to be ace sprinters . . . they are not expected to be able to run the 100 yards in even time. All they need is take-off speed.

So my tip to the budding young winger is to concentrate on sprinting over thirty yards . . . with special emphasis on the opening burst.

Terrific speed from a standing start gives you that advantage over a slow-turning full-back. Then you are away – and your soccer skill should do the rest.

The success of a winger also depends to a large extent on the smooth understanding with his inside-man. He must anticipate moves and be ready to switch inside and make quick, incisive passes.

The winger may be good in his own right, but a brilliant inside-forward can make him even better.

Take the case of Willie Hall, that great Tottenham and England inside-right. We developed such a wonderful understanding in a match with Ireland in 1938 that he scored five goals – all from my passes. I reckon I played better in that game because of the presence of Willie Hall. Stan Mortensen had the same ability to make a winger a headline player.

I have said that while a winger is now the No. 1 striker of the attack, he is also the prime provider of work for his three inside-forwards. So the accurate centre is still of supreme importance.

Don't waste centres. Make every one a telling weapon that can be charged with menace. Remember, the centre is for one of your forwards and should never go to the head or feet of a rival.

ATTACK FRUSTRATED

How many times do you see an attack frustrated because the winger lobs the ball harmlessly into the waiting and welcome hands of the goal-keeper?

Always make sure that the ball is pulled back to at least eight yards from the goal line. Always judge your cross so that it goes right to the head of a colleague. And, generally, aim for the far post.

This is a good plan because it forces defenders to turn in front of their goal – always a dangerous move. It gives a definite advantage to your own incoming forwards.

The same thing applies to corner kicks. How many are wasted in modern football? So many that you rarely see a goal scored from a corner kick these days. So pull the ball well back.

Accurate shooting is the new arm of the winger. But he must be dead on the target, for nine times out of ten he is shooting on an angle into a much narrower space.

I find the ideal way is to shoot for the far post, especially when the goal-keeper is coming at you. He is caught on the turn and cannot get back to stop the shot. The lob can also be used here to good effect.

But the winger can cause the greatest havoc with the quick back-pass from the goal line. It splits the goal wide open and brings many vital goals.

MENACING MOVE

I have often been accused of slowing down attacks because of my idea of taking the ball right down to the goal line. But I still think it is a most menacing move and well worth trying on occasions.

You see, the ball is pushed back to an advancing forward, generally unmarked, and he has the goal at his mercy. For the defenders are caught on the turn and before they can recover the ball is in the net.

This sort of back-pass won Blackpool the F.A. Cup at Wembley in 1953. And to my mind it will go on winning matches.

All this adds up to greater responsibility for the top-line winger in this modern world of football. It calls for more skill, speed, and a finer understanding of team play.

It makes the extreme winger the most dangerous man in the game. What a challenge for any boy who wants to make this part of football his career!

I Owe a Lot to Kicking a Tennis Ball

by Jimmy McIlroy

Jimmy McIlroy, who has won nearly 50 caps for Ireland, is one of the best ball-playing inside-forwards in the game and a giant in the Burnley side who has generously repaid the £8,000 fee paid to Glentoran in 1950 for his services. Left Burnley to help Stoke City win promotion.

IT is a fallacy that I refuse to acknowledge the benefits of coaching, because any success I've merited is due in no small measure to the hours of coaching I've received since I first kicked a ball in a little Irish village.

I believe that I, and any coach, can improve a boy's knowledge of football.

The greatest inside-forwards I've known weren't necessarily the best ball-players, although it's a tremendous advantage to have complete control of the ball, to kill it dead in an instant, and be able to use both feet easily and accurately.

I'm certain I owe a lot to countless hours spent kicking a tennis ball against the wall of my home, when my pals tired of soccer, and using my imagination as an opponent, conjured up all sorts of incidents I was likely to encounter in a match, such as a defender rushing in to tackle and being forced to play the ball first-time from all heights and angles. I'm convinced this "self-coaching" developed my skills, timing, and balance, because in my imaginative wonderland I captured the pace and excitement of a real game, and it's only in matches skills are nurtured into peak performances.

It's possible, too, Irish as it may sound, that I was fortunate my schooldays happened during the war years, when footballs were practically non-existent, and touch and ball-sense was fostered with the only balls occasionally available—tennis balls. On the other hand, today's young footballers have much better facilities, better playing surfaces, proper footballs, and with the professional footballer's lot vastly improved, there is a wonderful incentive to make the grade in the game. Well-meaning people with a limited knowledge of soccer, used to pass on advice and coaching in my very early teens; tips such as, shoot often on greasy surfaces or get rid quickly against rugged opponents. All of which was well meant, but useless at the time, because I played football according to instinct and was solely concerned in playing the only way I knew how.

Even at seventeen, and a professional with the Irish league club Glentoran, I can't remember absorbing much of the tactics or team talks prior to every match.

By Irish standards I was playing so well that in March, 1950, at the age of 18, Burnley bought me for £8,000, and it wasn't until arriving in England that I realized how much of the game I still had to learn. Football is similar to any professional career, in that, years of study and experience, or to be more explicit, years of playing, thinking, and talking amongst footballers are needed, before a boy feels he knows a little of what his job is all about.

Naturally every team position is important, but that of inside-forward is vital. Here is usually found the brains of the side, the schemer, who if partnered by a goal-snatching inside-forward, go a long way towards forming the nucleus of a good team.

Generally, inside-forwards are classed in one of two categories – the striker and the schemer, his type of style being determined by the boy's make-up, or character.

I enjoy playing behind the other four forwards, just in front of my wing-halves, where I try to position so as to receive the ball from them and then, either with a first-time pass, or by holding it for a few seconds to enable a colleague to run into an attacking position, and a way to goal may be created if passed accurately.

Deep-lying inside-forwards need stamina to cover the entire field for 90 minutes, confidence to hold the ball long enough until someone takes up an advantageous position and courage to keep on looking for it when things aren't going well.

If a boy thirsts for goals, as Jimmy Greaves does, he becomes a striker, and I don't expect him to burn up his energy seeking the ball. He must save himself for those lightning sprints and darts around the penalty area in his quest for goals. What a lot of people fail to realize is just how strength-sapping those sprints are, which leads to this type of inside-forward often being called lazy. Nevertheless, if my poaching partner scores week after week, I don't grumble about running a few extra yards for him.

Trying to blot inside-forwards out of the game are the wing-halves. Some are highly skilled, often poor tacklers, but brilliant ball-players and clever at starting attacks. Others are noted more for their defensive assets, their tackling and positional play.

A good team has one of each type, and I prefer to oppose the footballing wing-half, because he allows me that yard extra in which to receive the ball and control it, and it turns out to be a test of skill, not one of strength and stamina.

His counterpart tackles hard, sometimes too hard for my liking, marks closely and on the whole is a spoiler. When opposite this type I'm happy if I have my regular wing-half behind me, with Burnley it's Jimmy Adamson, with Ireland, Danny Blanchflower, both great players, both of whom I've played with so long as to be able to almost read each other's thoughts.

If they see I'm tightly marked, they hold the ball whilst I sprint away from them, taking my opponent with me, until I reverse sharply, gaining enough space to collect their pass. Or, I draw him on to the wing or into the centre, leaving a space for Jimmy or Danny to surge forward. Adamson and I have spent years talking, planning, and plotting to reach the understanding we have.

In our early days at Turf Moor we were encouraged to work out moves together by our two trainers Bill Dougall and Ray Bennion, but half the time we coached each other. Ray and Bill introduced us to new skills, such as, hitting a "dipper" (a shot that drops suddenly due to top-spin), dribbling by stepping over the ball from side to side, and shielding it from an opponent with the body.

I respect these veteran coaches simply because they were experienced enough to know that for each individual certain skills came naturally and easily, and they never insisted we relentlessly attempted the ones we disliked.

I believe in showing a boy in his teens everything I can do with a ball, encouraging him to discover in as many ways as possible that the ball can be played by all parts of the body, and allowing him to pursue the skills which appeal to him.

Whether as a striker or a schemer, one thing is essential – fitness. To the ambitious youngster this is the easiest part of football to attain, or perhaps I should say, it should be. Any boy who loves the game won't have to be bullied into reaching peak fitness. He should derive immense pleasure and pride from the feeling of fitness; his game will benefit and the satisfaction gained in out-running an opponent will be worth that extra bit of training he had to grit his teeth to withstand. For me, the pre-season training is the worst. When all those surplus pounds collected during the summer break have to be "lost", and the emphasis is on "pressure" and "circuit" training. Still it's the modern trend and anyway it only lasts a few weeks until we are back at the type of training I like best – five-a-side.

Five-a-side is the finest practice I can think of. It produces every move in the game; it can be conditioned to make players part quickly, improve their stamina, and make them think and move quickly in a narrow space.

There are many ways to fitness, but boys must realize that training doesn't finish at the ground. All the good work can be nullified by lack of thought, at home, in a snooker room, etc. Too much food, not enough sleep and fresh air are examples of the harm a young footballer can do himself, but if he really loves soccer, his determination to reach the top will provide the will-power to resist all temptations.

Alfredo di Stefano

Real Madrid centre-forward, talks in an interview with Gordon Ross

This world famous centre-forward of Real Madrid has been considered by the critics as the finest player in Europe. He came to Real from the Argentine as an experienced International and has since won over 30 caps for Spain. English followers saw him give a superb display of artistry for Real Madrid against Arsenal at Highbury in September, 1962.

Question: How old were you when you first became interested in football and where and when did you start playing?

Answer: I started playing in Buenos Aires, when I was seven or eight years old, in small insignificant football grounds.

Question: What coaching did you have when you first began?

Answer: At school I had to train twice a week in gymnastics and ball control. I was then ten or twelve years old.

Question: Did you start your career as a centre-forward?

Answer: I started playing as outside-right.

Question: How much did you practise and how did you practise?

Answer: I practised as the professional teams did. In the afternoon I played football with friends in small football grounds that we had in our part of town. When night fell we continued playing by the light of the street lamps. I practised with balls of paper, rags, stones, orange peel, banana peel, in fact anything that it is possible to kick.

Question: How much did you practise heading?

Answer: Enough to know how to head the ball.

Question: How did you practise shooting?

Answer: Usually at the end of training, 15 or 20 minutes nearly every day.

Question: What methods have you used to keep fit throughout your career?

Answer: A healthy life and having the luck to be able to
count on good coaches during the whole of my
life. These are definitely the ones who taught me
how to keep myself in good shape, making me
train enthusiastically.

Question: What have you found the most difficult thing
to do?

Answer: Shoot corners with the left foot.

Question: When you are playing in a match how quickly
can you see any weaknesses the centre-half opposing you may have and how do you take advantage
of these?

Answer: Generally you know how your adversary plays.
If he likes to dribble, if he heads the ball well
or not, etc. When you discover one of these
weaknesses, it is at that special point that you
must attack.

Question: Would you alter your tactics if the centre-half
was very tall?

Answer: Usually tall men have very little flexibility at the
waist so you try to go to the opposite side to which
you intend to pass.

Question: Who is the best centre-half you have played
against and why?

Answer: The best centre-half that I have known was Raul
Pini (Uruguay) whom I played with for the
"Millionaires of Bogota". He was the perfect
player. He had technique, speed, headed the ball
very well, knew how to clear the ball long or
short whichever he pleased, he was an amazing
dribbler, in fact, he was complete.

Question: Why do you think Real Madrid has been so
successful over such a long period?

Answer: First of all (and this is my opinion because many
years passed by without them enjoying success)
when they became successful the directors of the
Club maintained the Club spirit and harmony
by looking for new players and blending them

little by little into the team so that there were no great changes fundamentally. This is in my opinion what Real Madrid has done to keep at the top of the football world for such a long time.

Question: How is Spanish football different from other countries?

Answer: Spanish football consists of a speed and inspiration that generally brings out the best in a man as a footballer, more so than learning about tactics and strategies from books.

Question: Would a boy in Spain get as much chance of playing football and being coached as he would in England?

Answer: No, because in Spain the training methods are inferior. The reason being that there are not as many facilities such as Clubs and grounds, nor are there as many amateurs as you have in England.

Question: How do you spend the time on the day of a match and what do you eat?

Answer: Usually the matches are played in the afternoons. I get up the day of the match at about 9 o'clock in the morning, I then have a hot cup of coffee, and toast, go for a short walk, read the newspapers, and at 12 noon I eat lunch with the rest of the team. This consists of two consommé, ham, a steak, stewed fruit, and coffee. Then I go to bed until an hour-and-a-half before the game (that's when we have to go to the stadium). After the game I take a hot bath, have a light meal, and then sleep.

Question: Do you call for the ball in a match?

Answer: Yes, all the ninety minutes of the game.

Question: How do you like the ball – in the air or on the ground?

Answer: I prefer the ball on the ground because it is less risky than in the air. In the air you have to dominate the ball and one is always more likely to receive more injuries and harder knocks.

153

Question: If a boy of about fifteen years of age who had played a lot of football asked you what advice you could give him to reach the top, what would you say?

Answer: My advice (and I have repeated it thousands of times) is that the boys dedicate themselves to learning ball control. Less gymnastics and more ball control. Gymnastics are fine when one is fifteen years old and if one wants to become an athlete, such as racing, jumping, marathon, etc., but for a boy who wants to dedicate himself to playing football, he must become an artist with the ball. It is the most important thing of all, to be able to do with the ball what you will.

Jack Clough, Cup Final Referee,

helps you with the finer points

One of the world's most experienced Referees, Jack Clough had handled a Cup Final as well as International matches of all denominations and in many countries.

It is surprising how little is known by the average football "fan" about the laws which govern the game of soccer.

Maybe I should admit that, in my own playing days, I was just as ignorant, but tuition to fit me for my job as referee made me realize just how limited had been my knowledge and secondly, how much more I enjoyed the spectacle when I became as mature as the official in charge.

It is certainly true that quite a number of professional players are sensitive and become irritable and reactive to unwise and vicious remarks uttered by so-called spectators. Few of these unkind individuals have ever played the game and in consequence know little of its hardships and trials. Their knowledge of football law is indeed small and constitutes a barrier which separates them completely from the true spirit and enjoyment of the game.

With the object of enabling the reader to enjoy the spectacle more fully, I think it would be interesting to examine some of the more confusing problems, and this article is prepared with the idea of extending your knowledge.

You will notice that all the points have been sectionalized under distinctive headings for simplicity of reading and ease of reference.

START OF PLAY

It is generally known that a coin is tossed prior to the start of any game, but I didn't anticipate that in Greece I would be handed two differently-coloured hard-boiled eggs to present to the captains as a substitute for the coin.

The idea was to crush them together and the captain who held the egg which didn't crack under impact won the "toss".

Don't ask me what happens if they both break under pressure. I can only assume that an unlimited supply of eggs was available for such emergencies.

But I don't think many of you will know that the captain

of the team winning the toss has the choice of kick-off or the direction in which he wishes to play; although I can only recall one instance in my career when the kick-off was chosen.

A very important point to remember about the kick-off – the ball must be played forward from the centre-spot, and is one of only two kicks in the game which must be played forward – the other being the penalty-kick.

PLAYERS' EQUIPMENT

Prior to setting the game into motion we have to consider players' equipment. Does it conform with the regulations? Is something being worn which could be considered a danger to opponents?

A player may be wearing a ring with a diamond setting which could prove highly dangerous. If so, it must be removed, or cushioned to avoid accidents.

Are boots well studded and without protruding nails?

These are all important issues and care must be taken to safeguard playing personnel from the risk of injury.

Apart from goal-keepers, some players wear headgear to cover hairless heads and I recall the centre-forward captain of the Cuban International side who graced a black beret for this purpose. It was certainly not dangerous, but a handicap to himself as he repeatedly retrieved it from the ground after dislodgement during the "brushes" of the game.

Plaster casts are also popular adornments in these modern times to cover broken wrists and hands, but I am strongly against permitting a man to play with a plaster cast. The limb is partially immobile and could present obvious danger to an opponent when they clash in the course of play. Again, we may find opponents rather reluctant to tackle a partially handicapped player and the sense of equality is removed. I am certainly convinced that the suppleness of a normal limb prevents many accidents, but when a limb is only partly controlled, accidents are quite likely to occur.

Spectacles can be worn by players, but they wear them at their own risk. Fortunately, the introduction of contact lenses has proved a boon to many players. These are concealed and cushion against the eye-ball with security, and no danger is associated to the wearer or his opponent. Wearers also assure me that they compare with a normal eye, during heavy rain and general inclement weather.

From the start of any game, instances will frequently arise when players of the same side shout instructions to each other or call for the ball to be passed to them.

It is a feature permitted under football law, always providing that it does not interfere with the play of an opponent.

Don't be one of those individuals who request the referee to stop this practice.

It is an important part of our modern game and managers and coaches encourage its wide use, and I personally feel that its introduction has greatly improved the pattern of the game.

It is designed to perfect movements and only on the rare occasions on which an opponent is distracted by the call will the referee penalize the shouting by the award of an indirect free-kick.

Bad language is, however, considered serious and, if uttered in a threatening or abusive manner to an opponent or official, it is classed under "violent conduct" and means dismissal from the field.

It is essential that we keep in the game the correct tone and essence of good conduct, but I have found that the occasions have been rare indeed when it has been necessary to check bad language.

GOAL-KEEPERS

In the region of the goal we come to the obvious "danger area", and it has certainly made the goal-keeper the topical man of the game.

Discussions are numerous and often heated, but, contrary to general opinion, a goal-keeper can be charged, even in his own goal-area, providing he is holding the ball. It is not, however, permissible to use the foot in trying to remove the ball from the "keeper's" grasp, and the wise referee will penalize this offence immediately.

Moving through the penalty-area the goal-keeper presents a difficult target, and the majority of offences committed by attacking forwards are due to bad timing on a moving "object".

I know that there are a great many of you who would like to see this charge outlawed, and I am in sympathy with this thought. Little satisfaction comes from it – merely bad temper and injury – but whilst it remains as a law it must be accepted.

Instances do arise when a goal-keeper, jumping for a high ball, swings in ape-like fashion from the crossbar. It is possible for a "keeper" to pull down the bar by 2–3 inches and restrict a scoring shot, and it is contrary to the laws. It is a case of ungentlemanly conduct and should be stamped out immediately it is introduced.

Most of you are aware that a goal-keeper, in possession of the ball, can take a maximum of four steps, after which he must release the ball from his hands. He can, of course, then recover the ball and take a further four steps, but touching the ball to the ground without release of his hold is not fulfilling the law – he is still in possession.

Any goal-keeper who constantly prowls around the penalty area, taking sequences of four steps and then bouncing the ball, as we frequently observe on the Continent, is often doing so with the object of wasting time, when a winning position is held. This is ungentlemanly conduct and must be penalized by the award of an indirect free-kick and it quickly brings the transgressor into line.

Remember also that if the goal-keeper leaves the penalty area whilst still holding the ball he becomes a normal player and is guilty of handling.

INJURY

When injury is sustained by a player, play is only stopped if the referee considers the injury to be of a serious nature.

Sometimes it is difficult to define, as many players display great fortitude after receiving an injury, whilst others seek immediate attention; but if doubt exists a stoppage of play will be made and the trainer called to give treatment.

The Football Association, however, make it clear that if an injury of a minor nature is received, treatment should not be given on the field and you will note instances of players being directed to the touch-line for treatment, even whilst play is continuing.

It will also be seen that, after off-field treatment, a player can re-enter the field whilst play is in progress, providing he receives a signal from, or reports to, the referee.

The wise object of these regulations is an attempt by the Football Association to reduce stoppages to a minimum.

FREE-KICKS

A feature which causes considerable discussion is the quickly taken free-kick.

The free-kick is meant to be of advantage to the side receiving the award and the quickness of the re-start should always be encouraged, providing the ball is stationary and in the vicinity of the place where the offence occurred.

We still notice a few players who have adopted the unsporting habit of standing over, or close to, the ball, when an opponent is preparing to take a free-kick. The intention is one of causing delay and to enable defenders to consolidate their positions. The referee must caution a player for this offence and, once this keenness is shown, I am certain the practice will soon die a quite natural death.

Many spectators are unable to identify the difference between a direct free-kick, from which a goal can be scored direct, and an indirect one, when the ball must be played a second time by another player before a goal can be scored.

With the object of clarifying the position, the F.A. suggest that, when an indirect free-kick is awarded, the referee should signify this by raising one hand above his head. Don't ridicule him – he doesn't seek permission to leave the field, but merely indicates to both player and spectator that a goal cannot be scored direct from the initial kick.

The idea is a good one and gives the spectator a direct contact with the control of the game.

ADVANTAGE

"A referee will not penalize any offence if by so doing he gives advantage to the offending team."

On many occasions you will see a player tripped and yet he recovers and proceeds with the ball and the referee instinctively waves on play.

This is good refereeing and I delight in seeing a game under perfect control with the advantage law applied to its maximum. It brings a smoothness of pattern which most spectators appreciate and adds charm to a game, which otherwise could be completely ruined by unwise and unnecessary halting of the play.

GAMESMANSHIP

Gamesmanship is a term applied to habits of an unsporting nature, not considered to be associated with the true "spirit of the game".

"Persistent appealing in an effort to undermine authority" – "Wasting time" – "Stealing yards at the taking of a throw or a free-kick" are some of the methods adopted.

But there are other forms, many introduced with a great deal of cunning, and referees are ever watchful for any new methods being attempted.

I must agree that a particular blade of grass is not essential for the placing of the ball at a free-kick, nor a few inches at the throw, but any player intentionally "stealing yards" should be subjected to discipline.

All these acts are designed to waste valuable time and do considerable harm to the game.

The referee will treat them seriously and it is within his power to warn a player for offences of this nature and, if repeated, caution or dismiss him from the field.

LINESMEN

The linesmen's duties are very clearly defined – they are employed to assist.

Largely do they figure in offside decisions when their positioning should enable them, with considerable ease, to indicate to the referee a player in this position.

It is usual for them also to signify when a ball goes out of play, but a good linesman will work with a referee and bring to his notice any infringement which he knows the referee has not seen.

They are not empowered to give decisions and will not endeavour to dominate the game with undue interference.

The referee may decide that he does not require guidance from a flagging linesman, so you would be wise to listen for the whistle, rather than watch the flag.

I like to see a happy and confident team of officials – men who treat the game as a pleasure, and even though their duties are serious and important, they don't let these responsibilities spoil their enjoyment.

OBSTRUCTION

Obstruction may seem a little confusing to many football supporters and in certain instances a player is wrongly thought to be guilty of this offence, when his movement is within the law.

It is often seen that a player will shield the ball, which is within his playing distance, from an opponent, with the intention of allowing it to run over goal or touch-line. Providing he makes no attempt to restrict his opponent from reaching the ball, this would be permitted. He could, however, back into his opponent with the obvious intention of checking him. This would be a case of obstruction, and, if the player offended against did not use the privilege allowed to him of charging his opponent in the back, a free-kick for obstruction would be given.

Unfortunately we have creeping into the game the action of some players who step into the path of an opponent to prevent him from playing the ball. It is a habit which the Continentals use with frequency against British teams and is a distasteful form of bad sportsmanship.

We are fortunate that it has not become firmly established in these islands, and I am convinced that the wisdom of club officials and firm action by the referees will keep it subdued.

OFFSIDE

Offside is not the confusing feature that many people imagine.

If a player *at the moment the ball is last played* is (a) in his own half of the field, (b) has two opponents between himself and their goal-line, or (c) is behind the ball – he cannot be offside.

Remember that the player's position is determined at the moment the ball is last played by a member of his side.

Players often drift in and out of "offside positions" during the course of a game but they are not penalized because they are so remote from a movement that they are not considered to be interfering with the play.

The only disturbing feature in the offside law is the "played on" part which is confusing, vexing, and indeed debatable.

Condensed it is an application of common sense. Even though a player may be in an offside position and not apparently interfering with play, if his presence in this position prompts a defender to reach for a ball which he normally would not attempt to play, a decision of offside should be given. The attacker is in an advantageous position and quite likely seeking an advantage and he should be penalized.

Think of it from the sensible angle and you will find that you are, quite often, in agreement with the referee.

Incidentally, a player cannot be offside from a goal-kick, corner-kick, a throw-in, or a dropped ball.

HANDLING

A player is guilty of a handling offence if he *intentionally* carries, strikes, or propels the ball with his hand or arm.

Note the word *intentional*, and, however unfortunate it may sometimes appear, unless deliberation is associated with hand or arm contact no offence has been committed.

It is also essential to remember that the area associated with handling extends from the tips of the fingers, along the whole length of the arm to its link with the shoulder.

I consider that far too frequently a player is penalized when the ball touches his hand or arm through no intentional action of his own.

THROW-IN

At the point where the ball crosses the touch-line it must be thrown-in and at the moment of delivery the thrower must face the field of play, with part of each foot either on or behind the touch-line.

It must be thrown from *over* the head, so that any position from behind to the top of the head will be allowed, always providing the ball is thrown and not dropped.

Many players attempt to throw the ball from the running track and in one case I saw a player fling it from amongst spectators in the paddock, but this should not be allowed.

Position is important and, as the rule states that the ball is in play immediately it is thrown, the vicinity of the touch-line is the place from where it must be taken.

Both hands must be employed when throwing the ball and used with equality. It is not permitted for a player, with the idea of gaining additional impetus, to throw the ball with one hand and guide it with the other.

SHOULDER CHARGE

Unfortunately, the shoulder charge, between players (distinct from goal-keepers) is one of the attractive features which appears to be declining in present day football, and to me it is unfortunate.

When the obstruction law was clarified and charging penalized (however fair) unless a player was attempting to play the ball, a grave fear of the punishment likely to be imposed became an obsession to players, and most of them now appear to avoid body contact.

The law was never altered, merely more publicity being given to the existing law on obstruction, but it scared many officials and, in consequence, charging appears to be drifting from the game.

It is a pity that this situation should arise; it was never intended to outlaw the charge and most of you will agree that timed with neatness and precision, charging is one of the charms of the game.

GENERAL

Always remember that the boundary lines are part of the field of play and the ball is not out of play until it has *wholly and completely* crossed the line.

It will also be noticed that a stoppage of the play will be made without any breach of law (such as injury), and the ball will be dropped to re-start the game. It is not considered in play until it touches the ground and if played before it has done so, it must again be dropped.

Instances will often arise of dangerous play – "stooping much too low to head the ball" – "kicking at the ball in a way that may present danger to an opponent" – "kicking the ball from the goal-keeper's hands" – are all common offences, but all cases of dangerous play are punishable by the award of an indirect free-kick.

It is so very difficult trying to cover the whole of the regulations in an article of this nature, as so many intricate and debatable points arise.

The major features have, however, been covered, and any spectator who will take a little time to familiarize himself with the fundamental points will find that it greatly improves his judgement and his pleasure.

The pattern of the game will become clearer, the spectacle brighter, and if some of the points mentioned have assisted in your "education" I am certain that the result will prove beneficial to your enjoyment.

Fact and Curiosity

CLIFF BASTIN, of Arsenal, before the end of the 1930–31 season, had achieved the unique distinction of becoming an England International and collecting F.A. Cup winning and First Division Championship medals before he was twenty years old.

* * *

Newcastle United took the F.A. Cup with them on a tour of South Africa in 1952 – the first time that the much-prized trophy had left the British Isles.

* * *

Neil McBain kept goal for New Brighton against Hartlepools United on March 15th, 1947 – four months after his 52nd birthday.

* * *

Of the original twelve Football League Clubs in 1888 only three have played in the Competition in every subsequent season, including both war periods. They are Bolton Wanderers, Burnley, and Everton.

* * *

Middlesbrough were beaten 9–0 by Blackburn Rovers on November 6th, 1954, and kept the same team the following week.

* * *

Horace Blew, whose only appearance with Manchester United in the 1905–06 season was in an away match on Good Friday against Chelsea, won a medal for this one game. The point won in that drawn game helped United to win promotion.

Five clubs from the same County finished the 1914–15 season as the first five clubs in the First Division. They were Everton, Oldham Athletic, Blackburn Rovers, Burnley, and Manchester City.

* * *

Tom Pearson, when he was Newcastle United's outside-left, played for England against Scotland in a war-time International in 1939, and represented Scotland against England in a full International in 1947.

* * *

David Walsh scored for West Bromwich Albion in all the first six Football League matches of his career early in the 1946–47 season.

* * *

A goal-scoring goal-keeper! Arnold Birch, Chesterfield's goal-keeper, scored five times from the penalty spot in the 1923–24 season.

* * *

In 1942 Alf Ramsey and Harry Evans both signed for Southampton on the same day. On August 9th, 1955, both became Managers for the first time – Ramsey with Ipswich Town and Evans with Aldershot.

* * *

Birmingham City (then Small Heath) were the first Association Football Club to become a Limited Liability Company, in 1888.

* * *

A football manager's job these days is fraught with problems, but what about David Steele, who for a time managed two Clubs at the same time. He left Bradford to become Huddersfield Town's Manager in September, 1943. For some weeks until Bradford appointed a new Manager Steele controlled the fortunes of both Clubs.

Fourteen Football League grounds were damaged by bombing during the last war – Arsenal, Birmingham City, Charlton Athletic, Manchester United, Sheffield United, Fulham, Sunderland, Leicester City, Notts County, West Ham United, Leyton Orient, Millwall, Plymouth Argyle, and New Brighton.

* * *

When Chesterfield played Accrington Stanley in 1930 all three of Chesterfield's half-backs scored, Horace Wass, Harold Wightman, and Dick Duckworth, a case without parallel in Football League history.

* * *

Six players who figured in the same position with Football League Clubs in London have represented England in Test match cricket – Patsy Hendren (Brentford), Leslie Ames (Clapton Orient), John Arnold (Fulham), Laurie Fishlock (Millwall), Bill Edrich (Tottenham Hotspur) and Denis Compton (Arsenal). All of them played at outside-left.

* * *

George Camsell, who scored 59 goals for Middlesbrough in 1926–27, hit nine hat-tricks during that season.

* * *

Fred Hopkin, an outside-left with Liverpool, failed to score a single goal in 133 appearances between 1921 and 1928.

* * *

The late W. H. Smith, former England outside-left, was the first player to score a goal direct from a corner-kick. He did so when playing for Huddersfield Town against Arsenal in 1924. The rule making such a feat possible had only been introduced in the previous June.

* * *

The first half-time scoreboard ever erected on a Football League ground was at Middlesbrough in 1902. The first

news it showed was that Middlesbrough were winning an
away match in 1902.

* * *

A triple success has made George Stephenson the holder of
a unique record. He was with Preston North End when
they were promoted to the First Division in 1933–34; with
Charlton Athletic the next season when they rose to the
Second Division, and still with Charlton when they won
promotion to the First Division, one year later.

* * *

St. Johnstone, the Scottish team, are the only first-class Club
in either the Scottish League or the Football League
whose name contains the letter "J".

* * *

James Delaney appeared in the Final tie in the F.A. Cup,
the Scottish Cup, the Irish Cup, and the Eire Cup, with
Manchester United (1948), Glasgow Celtic (1937), Derry
City (1954), and Cork Athletic (1956).

* * *

Not since 1896–97 has a Football League team gone through
a complete season without drawing a single match.
Darwen did it by winning fourteen and losing sixteen of
their thirty Second Division matches in that season.

* * *

63,480 people paid nearly £7,000 to see an F.A. Cup-tie
between Newcastle United and Swansea Town in 1953.
It was abandoned because of fog after eight minutes play.

* * *

John Spuhler, Harry Bell, Ken Morton, Richard Davis, and
Tom Reynolds formed Darlington's forward line in
1955–56. All five of them had previously played with
Sunderland.

Darlington, in 1910–11, are the only Club to have reached the last sixteen in the F.A. Cup after playing through all the Qualifying Rounds.

* * *

In a Second Division game against Chelsea in 1912 the Glossop goal-keeper, Butler, saved a penalty kick, but in doing so had stepped forward and the kick was ordered to be re-taken. Butler protested so vigorously that he was sent off the field, and another player, Cuffe, went in to goal to face the second kick.

* * *

John Hewie, Charlton Athletic, had never been to Scotland before he played for Scotland against England at Hampden Park on April 14th, 1956. Hewie was born in South Africa and his father in Scotland.

* * *

An extraordinary F.A. Cup coincidence was the meeting between Leeds United and Cardiff City in three successive seasons, all three at Leeds, and Cardiff winning all three by the same score – 2–1. The seasons were 1955–56, 1956–57, and 1957–58.

* * *

All five forwards in the Welsh International team against Ireland in 1953 – Medwin, Charles, Ford, Allchurch, and Griffiths – were born in Swansea and had played for Swansea Town.

* * *

Charlton Athletic's team against Preston North End in 1953 contained five South Africans – Hewie, Chamberlain, O'Linn, Leary, and Firmani.

* * *

Billy Meredith was within three months of being 47 when he was transferred from Manchester United to Manchester City at the end of the 1920–21 season.

Can you imagine an England team playing for twenty minutes with only ten men because one of its players was late in arriving? It happened in 1879. W. E. Clegg, chosen to play for England against Wales at the Oval, was engaged in preparing evidence for the trial of Charlie Peace. He had to work late on the case and was unable to leave Sheffield for London on the Friday night. Next morning his train was delayed by heavy snow and the match had been in progress for twenty minutes before Clegg appeared.

*   *   *

Shooting for goal when playing in a Second Division match against Burnley in 1936, Chesterfield's centre-forward, Walter Ponting saw the ball burst and fail to reach the net.

*   *   *

A total of 202,343 people watched a thrice-played Fifth Round F.A. Cup-tie between Aston Villa and Charlton Athletic in 1938 – 76,031 at Charlton, 61,530 at Villa Park, and 64,782 at Highbury.

*   *   *

Six goals, all for offside, were disallowed in a Third South match between Swindon Town and Southend United in 1949.

*   *   *

When Portsmouth won the Football League Championship in 1948–49 the side did not contain one International.

*   *   *

Twenty-two goals in two matches between Oldham Athletic and Tranmere Rovers on Christmas and Boxing Day, 1935, must constitute a record. Oldham scored four goals in each match. They won the first 4–1 and lost the second 4–13.

*   *   *

Andrew Smailes, whom Rotherham United signed on a month's trial in August, 1929, stayed with the Club for twenty-nine years. He became trainer in 1933, manager in 1952, and left the Club in October, 1958.

* * *

Harry Storer, as Manager, signed the same player three times for different Clubs. He signed Martin McDonnell for Birmingham City in May, 1947; for Coventry City in October, 1949; and for Derby County in July, 1955.

* * *

Four half-backs with Wolverhampton Wanderers all played for England in 1958 – Clamp, Wright, Slater, and Flowers.

* * *

White, Kilmarnock's left-half, took a penalty kick seven times against Partick Thistle in 1945. Six times he shot and the referee ruled that Partick's goal-keeper had moved each time. With the seventh attempt the referee was satisfied . . . so was the goal-keeper. He saved the shot!

* * *

Peter Dobing once had the unique experience of being selected for both teams who were playing each other on the same day. As a junior he was invited to sign amateur forms for both Blackburn Rovers and Manchester United. Both picked him for an "A" Team match when the two Clubs were playing each other. Dobing solved a tricky problem by not playing for either.

* * *

Arsenal won the F.A. Cup in 1950 by playing seven matches in London. They beat Sheffield Wednesday, Swansea Town, Burnley, and Leeds United at Highbury; travelled a few miles down the road to meet Chelsea in the Semi-Final and a Semi-Final replay, and then to Wembley to beat Liverpool.

James McGuire who played for Northampton from 1932–37 became President of the American Soccer League in 1950.

*   *   *

Bob Etheridge became a Bristol City player in September, 1956, and an hour later was a professional with Gloucestershire County Cricket Club.

*   *   *

Wilfred Minter, playing for St. Albans City against Dulwich Hamlet in a replayed Cup-tie in 1922 scored seven goals. . . . His team lost 7–8!

*   *   *

Almost on half-time in a match between Middlesbrough and Lincoln City in 1958, Lincoln City were awarded a penalty-kick. The referee allowed extra time for it to be taken but Chapman's shot was parried by the Lincoln goal-keeper. Chapman dashed up to try and score from the rebound but the referee blew the whistle for half-time before he could take a second shot at goal.

*   *   *

A Manager once signed a player for two Clubs who failed to play a single game under his management. Norman Dodgin signed Andrew Torrance for Yeovil Town in the summer of 1957, but became Manager of Barrow before the following season started. At the end of the season 1957–58 Dodgin signed Torrance for Barrow, and became Oldham Athletic's Manager shortly afterwards.

*   *   *

What advantage is it to score first in a football match? The following results make you wonder. Middlesbrough scored first, but lost 1–8 to Charlton Athletic in September, 1958, and Nottingham Forest scored first against Birmingham City in 1959 and lost 1–7.

Luton Town, beaten Cup Finalists in the 1958–59 season, had an average home attendance during the season of 19,872 – the smallest in the First Division.

* * *

Billy Gray, later with Nottingham Forest, played in two matches on the same day and was on the winning side each time. He played an away Football Combination match for Leyton Orient Reserves on the morning of Monday, December 27th, 1948, and a home Third Division game with Orient against Port Vale in the afternoon. Something similar happened with two Arsenal players, Jack Kelsey and Danny Clapton, playing in an afternoon International match between England and Wales in Birmingham. They raced back to London afterwards and appeared for Arsenal against the Italian Club, Juventus, Kelsey for the whole match, and Clapton coming on as a substitute at half-time.

* * *

Three Football League professionals have won the Edinburgh Powderhall Sprint. James Cowan (Aston Villa) in the 1890s, Tom Eatock, Bolton Wanderers, 1920, and James Harley, Liverpool, 1936.

* * *

In April, 1936, Harry Wait was Walsall's first team goal-keeper, and his son, H. G. Wait, was in goal for Walsall's Reserves on the same day.

* * *

Giant-killers in the F.A. Cup are the great fascination of the competition. In the Third Round in 1951, twelve ties were won by teams playing opposition of a higher status to themselves.

* * *

The town of Bolton has supplied three Referees who have officiated in the Cup Final – J. T. Howcroft (1920), A. E. Fogg (1935), and J. H. Clough (1959).

Tony McNamara played in all four Divisions of the Football League within a space of twelve months. Everton (First), Liverpool (Second), Crewe Alexandra (Fourth), and Bury (Third). All between September, 1957, and September, 1958.

* * *

Just before the 1914–18 war, Tom Revill played for Derbyshire at cricket and Chesterfield and Stoke City at football. His son, Alan, has played for Derbyshire and Leicestershire at cricket and Sheffield United at football.

* * *

The name Major Marindin would mean little to modern followers of football – yet he holds a football record – he has refereed the Cup Final more than any other referee. In 1879–80 and then all the seven from 1883–84 to 1889–90 inclusive.

* * *

When Sunderland were elected to the Football League in 1890 they put a notice over the entrance to their ground which read "We have arrived and we are staying here". They stayed in the First Division until 1958.

* * *

William Richardson, the West Bromwich Albion centre-forward, scored four goals in four minutes against West Ham United on November 7th, 1931, and three in five minutes against Derby County on September 10th, 1933. Because there were two William Richardsons he was given the second initial of G. The "G" stood for "Ginger"!

* * *

It was once said of Ronnie Allen of West Bromwich Albion that when he took a penalty kick he liked something to aim at, and had an arrangement with a local press photographer that he would position himself behind the goal when Allen was taking a penalty and Allen would aim at the camera. On one occasion the ball burst on its way to the goal. The photographer had the scoop picture of the year.

On the first day of the 1956–57 season, on August 18th, a match between Tranmere Rovers and Workington was abandoned because of the weather . . . a cloudburst struck the ground and the match was called off at half-time.

* * *

David Halliday of Sunderland scored his 100th First Division goal on March 10th, 1928, in only his 101st match.

* * *

Newmarket Town Football Club were presented with a flag by the Eastern Counties Football League in 1952. Their record for the season – Played 34 games; lost 34 games, they scored 19 goals and had 171 scored against them. The flag was given in appreciation of the sporting way in which Newmarket accepted defeat every Saturday in the season.

* * *

At the start of the 1959–60 season, right-back Gerald Baker, though only twenty the previous April, had been with Bradford longer than any of his playing colleagues.

* * *

There is a unique case of a Sunday League becoming affiliated to the Football Association, which did not recognize Sunday play. The Birmingham Monday League were granted permission during the war to run a Sunday section to meet the needs of war-time factory workers.

* * *

The Sunderland forward-line of 1953–54 contained Internationals of four countries. Bingham (Ireland), Wright (Scotland), Ford (Wales), Shackleton or Watson (England), and Elliott (England).

* * *

When Manchester United won the Cup in 1948 they had to beat six First Division Clubs to do it – Aston Villa,

Liverpool, Charlton Athletic, Preston North End, Derby County, and Blackpool.

* * *

Portsmouth were promoted to the First Division instead of Manchester City in 1927 because of a better goal average. How much better? . . . 0.0005 of a goal. On the last day of the season Manchester City won 8–0 but Portsmouth's 5–1 over Preston was just good enough.

* * *

Nottingham Forest beat Leicester Fosse 12–0 in a First Division League match in 1909. The Forest, at the time, were in danger of relegation, and after such a surprise result an inquiry was held. In the official findings it was mentioned that the Fosse players had attended the wedding celebration of a colleague on the previous day!

* * *

Have you ever seen one man face a whole football eleven? It happened some years ago in a London Professional Charity Fund Final, between Crystal Palace and Clapton (now Leyton) Orient. Played on the last day of the season the score after 90 minutes was 1–1. After an extra 15 minutes the score was still 1–1, and after a further 10 minutes. Then it happened. Ten Orient players had had enough, and walked off. One stayed, prepared to carry on alone, but Palace were awarded the match and the medals.

* * *

When Aston Villa played Derby County in 1946, a total of 76,588 people watched the game. When the famous Villa played their first match ever, the takings were five shillings and threepence.

* * *

When Arbroath once beat Bon Accord 36–0 in a Scottish Cup-tie, the Arbroath goal-keeper smoked his pipe throughout the match.

How many throw-ins would you think there are in the average football match? A careful check over a lengthy period shows the average number for first-class matches to be 85 – nearly one a minute.

* * *

How would you have liked to play football for Scotland? There would have been a great chance for you in 1873 when this official Scottish appeal was made; "International v. England" – Scotsmen desirous of playing are requested to send their names without delay to the Honorary Secretary, Scots XI.

* * *

Sunderland had a depressing start to the 1912 season. In the first seven matches they scored only two out of a possible fourteen points. How did they finish up? They won the League and reached the Cup Final.

* * *

Research over a long period has also shown that the most common result in League football is 2–1.

* * *

You often hear the poser, "Which was the first Club to take the F.A. Cup out of England?" The answer is Cardiff City, but when Bradford City won it in 1911 there were only two Englishmen in the side – there were eight Scots and an Irishman.

* * *

The world-famous Arsenal became a professional Club in 1891. Their first grandstand at Plumstead was a line of Army wagons, and their captain, David Danskin, the man who helped found the Club, took the money at the gate before leading his team out to play the match.

* * *

In 1893, a Tottenham Hotspur footballer named Payne lost his boots on the way home from a match, and a new pair was provided for him out of Club funds. The footballing powers-that-be at once declared that Payne, by accepting the gift, had relinquished amateur status, and the Club was suspended indefinitely from all competitions. The Club countered by turning professional, so that it is Mr. Payne's boots which put the world-famous Club where it is today!

* * *

Have you ever heard of a goal-keeper keeping goal at the same end throughout a match, and not changing over at half-time? It happened in Canada when Tottenham Hotspur were on tour and playing Saskatchewan. So superior were Spurs that they were leading 14–0 at half-time, so they lent Ditchburn to the home team. He kept the score down. The result was 18–1.

* * *

Just before the 1913 Cup Final Clem Stevenson of Aston Villa told Charlie Buchan of Sunderland, that his team would win and that Barber, the right-half, would score the only goal of the match. It happened . . . and not another goal was scored!

* * *

What about this for a football hazard? In the early days at The Dell, home of Southampton Football Club, an adjoining building was so close to the touch line that the wall had to be padded so that players would not injure themselves on the brickwork.

* * *

From the times of Edward II to Elizabeth, proclamations forbidding football were issued. The reason was that boys wasted their time and the games served merely as excuses for fighting.

* * *

Football transfer fees have now become astronomical. But what about J. Spelton of Mossend Celtic who was transferred to Holytown United at a fee of 30 corrugated sheets of iron, which Mossend urgently needed to fence in their ground.

* * *

In the early days of football, two umpires were appointed. These gentlemen, carrying sticks, patrolled one half of the field each, and gave an opinion only when appealed to by the players. They had no powers to penalize. If a player could not behave as a gentleman it was the other players who took action. He was not invited to play again. Hence the origin of the term "ungentlemanly conduct".

* * *

On their way to play in a Cup Final at the Crystal Palace in 1913, a weather-beaten old gypsy persuaded Sunderland's captain to cross her palm with silver. Jokingly, he asked her if his team would beat Aston Villa that afternoon. Her reply was that Sunderland would never win the Cup "until a Scottish lassie sits upon the throne of England". Nearly a quarter of a century passed before Sunderland reached the Final again in 1937, and Raich Carter received the Cup from the hands of the present Queen Mother, less than five months after that beloved "Scottish lassie" had come to the throne and only eleven days after her Coronation.

* * *

Touring Portugal in 1948 Arsenal were beaten by Oporto. The excitement of the Portuguese rose to such a height that it was decided to erect a monument to commemorate the occasion. A public subscription raised £20,000 and a fine monument to Arsenal's downfall now stands in the city.

Football Records

WORLD CUP WINNERS AND RUNNERS-UP

	Winners	Runners-up	Venue
1930	Uruguay	Argentina	Uruguay
1934	Italy	Czechoslovakia	Italy
1938	Italy	Hungary	France
1950	Uruguay	Brazil	Brazil
1954	Germany	Hungary	Switzerland
1958	Brazil	Sweden	Sweden
1962	Brazil	Czechoslovakia	Chile

INTERNATIONAL MATCHES
ENGLAND v. SCOTLAND

England won 28, Scotland won 33, Drawn 20

		England	Scotland
1872	Glasgow	0	0
1873	Kennington Oval	4	2
1874	Glasgow	1	2
1875	Kennington Oval	2	2
1876	Glasgow	0	3
1877	Kennington Oval	1	3
1878	Glasgow	2	7
1879	Kennington Oval	5	4
1880	Glasgow	4	5
1881	Kennington Oval	1	6
1882	Glasgow	1	5
1883	Sheffield	2	3
1884	Glasgow	0	1
1885	Kennington Oval	1	1
1886	Glasgow	1	1
1887	Blackburn	2	3
1888	Glasgow	5	0
1889	Kennington Oval	2	3
1890	Glasgow	1	1
1891	Blackburn	2	1
1892	Glasgow	4	0
1893	Richmond	5	2
1894	Glasgow	2	2
1895	Everton	3	0
1896	Glasgow	1	2

		England	Scotland
1897	Crystal Palace	1	2
1898	Glasgow	3	1
1899	Birmingham	2	1
1900	Glasgow	1	4
1901	Crystal Palace	2	2
1902	Birmingham	2	2
1903	Sheffield	1	2
1904	Glasgow	1	0
1905	Crystal Palace	1	0
1906	Glasgow	1	2
1907	Newcastle	1	1
1908	Glasgow	1	1
1909	Crystal Palace	2	0
1910	Glasgow	0	2
1911	Everton	1	1
1912	Glasgow	1	1
1913	Chelsea	1	0
1914	Glasgow	1	3
1920	Sheffield	5	4
1921	Glasgow	0	3
1922	Aston Villa	0	1
1923	Glasgow	2	2
1924	Wembley	1	1
1925	Wembley	1	1
1925	Glasgow	0	2
1926	Manchester	0	1
1927	Glasgow	2	1
1928	Wembley	1	5
1929	Glasgow	0	1
1930	Wembley	5	2
1931	Glasgow	0	2
1932	Wembley	3	0
1933	Glasgow	1	2
1934	Wembley	3	0
1935	Glasgow	0	2
1936	Wembley	1	1
1937	Glasgow	1	3
1938	Wembley	0	1
1939	Glasgow	2	1
1947	Wembley	1	1
1948	Glasgow	2	0
1949	Wembley	1	3
1950	Glasgow	1	0
1951	Wembley	2	3
1952	Glasgow	2	1
1953	Wembley	2	2
1954	Glasgow	4	2
1955	Wembley	7	2

		England	Scotland
1956	Glasgow	1	1
1957	Wembley	2	1
1958	Glasgow	4	0
1959	Wembley	1	0
1960	Glasgow	1	1
1961	Wembley	9	3
1962	Glasgow	0	2
1963	Wembley	1	2

ENGLAND v. WALES

England won 48, Wales won 11, Drawn 14

		England	Wales
1879	Kennington Oval	2	1
1880	Wrexham	3	2
1881	Blackburn	0	1
1882	Wrexham	3	5
1883	Kennington Oval	5	0
1884	Wrexham	4	0
1885	Blackburn	1	1
1886	Wrexham	3	1
1887	Kennington Oval	4	0
1888	Crewe	5	1
1889	Stoke-on-Trent	4	1
1890	Wrexham	3	1
1891	Sunderland	4	1
1892	Wrexham	2	0
1893	Stoke	6	0
1894	Wrexham	5	1
1895	Queen's Club, Kensington	1	1
1896	Cardiff	9	1
1897	Sheffield	4	0
1898	Wrexham	3	0
1899	Bristol	4	1
1900	Cardiff	1	1
1901	Newcastle	6	0
1902	Wrexham	0	0
1903	Portsmouth	2	1
1904	Wrexham	2	2
1905	Liverpool	3	1
1906	Cardiff	1	0
1907	Fulham	1	1
1908	Wrexham	7	1
1909	Nottingham	2	0
1910	Cardiff	1	0
1911	Millwall	3	0
1912	Wrexham	2	0
1913	Bristol	4	3

181

		England	Wales
1914	Cardiff	2	0
1920	Highbury	1	2
1921	Cardiff	0	0
1922	Liverpool	1	0
1923	Cardiff	2	2
1924	Blackburn	1	2
1925	Swansea	2	1
1926	Selhurst	1	3
1927	Wrexham	3	3
1927	Burnley	1	2
1928	Swansea	3	2
1929	Chelsea	6	0
1930	Wrexham	4	0
1931	Liverpool	3	1
1932	Wrexham	0	0
1933	Newcastle	1	2
1934	Cardiff	4	0
1935	Wolverhampton	1	2
1936	Cardiff	1	2
1937	Middlesbrough	2	1
1938	Cardiff	2	4
1946	Manchester	3	0
1947	Cardiff	3	0
1948	Aston Villa	1	0
1949	Cardiff	4	1
1950	Sunderland	4	2
1951	Cardiff	1	1
1952	Wembley	5	2
1953	Cardiff	4	1
1954	Wembley	3	2
1955	Cardiff	1	2
1956	Wembley	3	1
1957	Cardiff	4	0
1958	Aston Villa	2	2
1959	Cardiff	1	1
1960	Wembley	5	1
1961	Cardiff	1	1
1962	Wembley	4	0

ENGLAND v. IRELAND

England won 53, Ireland won 5, Drawn 12

		England	Ireland
1882	Belfast	13	0
1883	Liverpool	7	0
1884	Belfast	8	1
1885	Manchester	4	0
1886	Belfast	6	1

			England	Ireland
1887	Sheffield	....	7	0
1888	Belfast	....	5	1
1889	Everton	....	6	1
1890	Belfast	....	9	1
1891	Wolverhampton	....	6	1
1892	Belfast	....	2	0
1893	Birmingham	....	6	1
1894	Belfast	....	2	2
1895	Derby	....	9	0
1896	Belfast	....	2	0
1897	Nottingham	....	6	0
1898	Belfast	....	3	2
1899	Sunderland	....	13	2
1900	Dublin	....	2	0
1901	Southampton	....	3	0
1902	Belfast	....	1	0
1903	Wolverhampton	....	4	0
1904	Belfast	....	3	1
1905	Middlesbrough	....	1	1
1906	Belfast	....	5	0
1907	Everton	....	1	0
1908	Belfast	....	3	1
1909	Bradford	....	4	0
1910	Belfast	....	1	1
1911	Derby	....	2	1
1912	Dublin	....	6	1
1913	Belfast	....	1	2
1914	Middlesbrough	....	0	3
1919	Belfast	....	1	1
1920	Sunderland	....	2	0
1921	Belfast	....	1	1
1922	West Bromwich	....	2	0
1923	Belfast	....	1	2
1924	Everton	....	3	1
1925	Belfast	....	0	0
1926	Liverpool	....	3	3
1927	Belfast	....	0	2
1928	Everton	....	2	1
1929	Belfast	....	3	0
1930	Sheffield	....	5	1
1931	Belfast	....	6	2
1932	Blackpool	....	1	0
1933	Belfast	....	3	0
1934	Everton	....	2	1
1935	Belfast	....	3	1
1936	Stoke	....	3	1
1937	Belfast	....	5	1
1938	Manchester	....	7	0

		England	Ireland
1946	Belfast	7	2
1947	Everton	2	2
1948	Belfast	6	2
1949	Manchester	9	2
1950	Belfast	4	1
1951	Aston Villa	2	0
1952	Belfast	2	2
1953	Liverpool	3	1
1954	Belfast	2	0
1955	Wembley	3	0
1956	Belfast	1	1
1957	Wembley	2	3
1958	Belfast	3	3
1959	Wembley	2	1
1960	Belfast	5	2
1961	Wembley	1	1
1962	Belfast	3	1

ENGLAND v. ARGENTINA

		England	Argentina
1951	Wembley	2	1
1953	Buenos Aires	Abandoned	
1962	Rancagua, Chile (World Cup)	3	1

ENGLAND v. AUSTRIA

		England	Austria
1930	Vienna	0	0
1932	Chelsea	4	3
1936	Vienna	1	2
1951	Wembley	2	2
1952	Vienna	3	2
1958	Sweden (World Cup)	2	2
1961	Vienna	1	3
1962	Wembley	3	1

ENGLAND v. BELGIUM

		England	Belgium
1921	Brussels	2	0
1923	Highbury	6	1
1923	Antwerp	2	2
1924	West Bromwich	4	0
1926	Antwerp	5	3
1927	Brussels	9	1
1928	Antwerp	3	1
1929	Brussels	5	1
1931	Brussels	4	1
1936	Brussels	2	3

		England	Belgium
1947	Brussels	5	2
1950	Brussels	4	1
1952	Wembley	5	0
1954	Basle (World Cup)	4	4

ENGLAND v. BOHEMIA

		England	Bohemia
1908	Prague	4	0

ENGLAND v. BRAZIL

		England	Brazil
1956	Wembley	4	2
1956	Sweden (World Cup)	0	0
1959	Rio de Janeiro	0	2
1962	Vina Del Mar (World Cup) ...	1	3
1963	Wembley	1	1

ENGLAND v. BULGARIA

		England	Bulgaria
1957	Sofia	1	2
1962	Rancagua (World Cup) ...	0	0

ENGLAND v. CHILE

		England	Chile
1950	Rio de Janeiro	2	0
1953	Santiago	2	1

ENGLAND v. CZECHOSLOVAKIA

		England	Czechoslovakia
1934	Prague	1	2
1937	Tottenham	5	4
1963	Bratislava	4	2

ENGLAND v. DENMARK

		England	Denmark
1948	Copenhagen	0	0
1955	Copenhagen	5	1
1956	Wolverhampton	5	2
1957	Copenhagen	4	1

ENGLAND v. FINLAND

		England	Finland
1937	Helsinki	8	0
1956	Helsinki	5	1

ENGLAND v. FRANCE

		England	France
1923	Paris	4	1
1924	Paris	3	1
1925	Paris	3	2
1927	Paris	6	0
1928	Paris	5	1
1929	Paris	4	1
1931	Paris	2	5
1933	Tottenham	4	1
1938	Paris	4	2
1947	Highbury	3	0
1949	Paris	3	1
1951	Highbury	2	2
1955	Paris	0	1
1957	Wembley	4	0
1962	Sheffield (European Nations' Cup)	1	1
1963	Paris (European Nations' Cup)	2	5

ENGLAND v. GERMANY

		England	Germany
1930	Berlin	3	3
1935	Tottenham	3	0
1938	Berlin	6	3

ENGLAND v. WEST GERMANY

		England	West Germany
1954	Wembley	3	1
1956	Berlin	3	1

ENGLAND v. EAST GERMANY

		England	East Germany
1963	Leipzig	2	1

ENGLAND v. HOLLAND

		England	Holland
1935	Amsterdam	1	0
1946	Huddersfield	8	2

ENGLAND v. HUNGARY

		England	Hungary
1934	Budapest	1	2
1936	Highbury	6	2
1953	Wembley	3	6
1954	Budapest	1	7
1960	Budapest	0	2
1962	Rancagua (World Cup)	1	2

ENGLAND v. IRISH REPUBLIC

		England	Irish Republic
1946	Dublin	1	0
1949	Everton	0	2
1957	Wembley (World Cup)	5	1
1957	Dublin (World Cup)	1	1

ENGLAND v. ITALY

		England	Italy
1933	Rome	1	1
1934	Highbury	3	2
1939	Milan	2	2
1948	Turin	4	0
1949	Tottenham	2	0
1952	Florence	1	1
1959	Wembley	2	2
1961	Rome	3	2

ENGLAND v. LUXEMBOURG

		England	Luxembourg
1927	Luxembourg	5	2
1960	Luxembourg (World Cup)	9	0
1961	Highbury (World Cup)	4	1

ENGLAND v. MEXICO

		England	Mexico
1959	Mexico City	1	2
1961	Wembley	8	0

ENGLAND v. NORWAY

		England	Norway
1937	Oslo	6	0
1938	Newcastle	4	0
1949	Oslo	4	1

ENGLAND v. PERU

		England	Peru
1959	Lima	1	4
1962	Lima	4	0

ENGLAND v. PORTUGAL

		England	Portugal
1947	Lisbon	10	0
1950	Lisbon	5	3
1951	Everton	5	2
1955	Lisbon	1	3
1958	Wembley	2	1
1961	Lisbon	1	1
1961	Wembley	2	0

ENGLAND v. RUMANIA

		England	Rumania
1939	Bucharest	2	0

ENGLAND v. RUSSIA

		England	Russia
1958	Moscow	1	1
1958	Sweden (World Cup)	2	2
1958	Sweden (World Cup)	0	1
1958	Wembley	5	0

ENGLAND v. SPAIN

		England	Spain
1929	Madrid	3	4
1931	Highbury	7	1
1950	Rio de Janeiro (World Cup)	0	1
1955	Madrid	1	1
1955	Wembley	4	1
1960	Madrid	0	3
1960	Wembley	4	2

ENGLAND v. SWEDEN

		England	Sweden
1923	Stockholm	4	2
1923	Stockholm	3	1
1937	Stockholm	4	0
1947	Highbury	4	2
1949	Stockholm	1	3
1956	Stockholm	0	0
1959	Wembley	2	3

ENGLAND v. SWITZERLAND

		England	Switzerland
1933	Berne	4	0
1938	Zurich	1	2
1947	Zurich	0	1
1948	Highbury	6	0
1952	Zurich	3	0
1954	Berne	2	0
1962	Wembley	3	1
1963	Basle	8	1

ENGLAND v. URUGUAY

		England	Uruguay
1953	Montevideo	1	2
1954	Basle (World Cup)	2	4

ENGLAND v. U.S.A.

		England	U.S.A.
1950	Belo Horizonte (Brazil) (World Cup)	0	1
1953	New York	6	3
1959	Los Angeles	8	1

ENGLAND v. YUGOSLAVIA

		England	Yugoslavia
1939	Belgrade	1	2
1950	Highbury	2	2
1954	Belgrade	0	1
1956	Wembley	3	0
1958	Belgrade	0	5
1960	Wembley	3	3

F.A. CUP FINALS
1872 – 1963

* Indicates extra-time

Season	Winner	Runners-up	Score
AT THE OVAL			
1872	The Wanderers	bt Royal Engineers	1–0
AT LILLIE BRIDGE			
1873	The Wanderers	bt Oxford University	2–0
AT THE OVAL			
1874	Oxford University	bt Royal Engineers	2–0
1875	Royal Engineers	bt Old Etonians	1–1; 2–0
1876	The Wanderers	bt Old Etonians	0–0; 3–0
1877	The Wanderers	bt Oxford University	2–0*
1878	The Wanderers	bt Royal Engineers	3–1
1879	Old Etonians	bt Clapham Rovers	1–0
1880	Clapham Rovers	bt Oxford University	1–0
1881	Old Carthusians	bt Old Etonians	3–0
1882	Old Etonians	bt Blackburn Rovers	1–0
1883	Blackburn Olympic	bt Old Etonians	2–1*
1884	Blackburn Rovers	bt Queen's Park	2–1
1885	Blackburn Rovers	bt Queen's Park	2–0
1886	Blackburn Rovers	bt West Bromwich A.	0–0; 2–0
1887	Aston Villa	bt West Bromwich A.	2–0
1888	West Bromwich A.	bt Preston North End	2–1
1889	Preston North End	bt Wolverhampton W.	3–0
1890	Blackburn Rovers	bt Sheffield Wednesday	6–1
1891	Blackburn Rovers	bt Notts County	3–1
1892	West Bromwich A.	bt Aston Villa	3–0
AT MANCHESTER (FALLOWFIELD)			
1893	Wolverhampton W.	bt Everton	1–0
AT EVERTON			
1894	Notts County	bt Bolton Wanderers	4–1
AT CRYSTAL PALACE			
1895	Aston Villa	bt West Bromwich A.	1–0
1896	Sheffield Wednesday	bt Wolverhampton W.	2–1
1897	Aston Villa	bt Everton	3–2
1898	Nottingham Forest	bt Derby County	3–1
1899	Sheffield United	bt Derby County	4–1
1900	Bury	bt Southampton	4–0
1901	Tottenham Hotspur	bt Sheffield United	2–2; 3–1
1902	Sheffield United	bt Southampton	1–1; 2–1

Season	Winner	Runners-up	Score
1903	Bury	bt Derby County	6-0
1904	Manchester City	bt Bolton Wanderers	1-0
1905	Aston Villa	bt Newcastle United	2-0
1906	Everton	bt Newcastle United	1-0
1907	Sheffield Wednesday	bt Everton	2-1
1908	Wolverhampton W.	bt Newcastle United	3-1
1909	Manchester United	bt Bristol City	1-0
1910	Newcastle United	bt Barnsley	1-1; 2-0
1911	Bradford City	bt Newcastle United	0-0; 1-0
1912	Barnsley	bt West Bromwich A.	0-0;* 1-0
1913	Aston Villa	bt Sunderland	1-0
1914	Burnley	bt Liverpool	1-0

AT MANCHESTER (OLD TRAFFORD)

1915	Sheffield United	bt Chelsea	3-0

1916–1919   No competition owing to the war

AT STAMFORD BRIDGE

1920	Aston Villa	bt Huddersfield Town	1-0*
1921	Tottenham Hotspur	bt Wolverhampton W.	1-0
1922	Huddersfield Town	bt Preston North End	1-0

AT THE EMPIRE STADIUM, WEMBLEY

1923	Bolton Wanderers	bt West Ham United	2-0
1924	Newcastle United	bt Aston Villa	2-0
1925	Sheffield United	bt Cardiff City	1-0
1926	Bolton Wanderers	bt Manchester City	1-0
1927	Cardiff City	bt Arsenal	1-0
1928	Blackburn Rovers	bt Huddersfield Town	3-1
1929	Bolton Wanderers	bt Portsmouth	2-0
1930	Arsenal	bt Huddersfield Town	2-0
1931	West Bromwich A.	bt Birmingham	2-1
1932	Newcastle United	bt Arsenal	2-1
1933	Everton	bt Manchester City	3-0
1934	Manchester City	bt Portsmouth	2-1
1935	Sheffield Wednesday	bt West Bromwich A.	4-2
1936	Arsenal	bt Sheffield United	1-0
1937	Sunderland	bt Preston North End	3-1
1938	Preston North End	bt Huddersfield Town	1-0*
1939	Portsmouth	bt Wolverhampton W.	4-1
1940–45	No Competition owing to the war		
1946	Derby County	bt Charlton Athletic	4-1*
1947	Charlton Athletic	bt Burnley	1-0*
1948	Manchester United	bt Blackpool	4-2
1949	Wolverhampton W.	bt Leicester City	3-1
1950	Arsenal	bt Liverpool	2-0
1951	Newcastle United	bt Blackpool	2-0
1952	Newcastle United	bt Arsenal	1-0

Season	Winner	Runners-up	Score
1953	Blackpool	bt Bolton Wanderers	4–3
1954	West Bromwich A.	bt Preston North End	3–2
1955	Newcastle United	bt Manchester City	3–1
1956	Manchester City	bt Birmingham City	3–1
1957	Aston Villa	bt Manchester United	2–1
1958	Bolton Wanderers	bt Manchester United	2–0
1959	Nottingham Forest	bt Luton Town	2–1
1960	Wolverhampton W.	bt Blackburn Rovers	3–0
1961	Tottenham Hotspur	bt Leicester City	2–0
1962	Tottenham Hotspur	bt Burnley	3–1
1963	Manchester United	bt Leicester City	3–1

REPLAYED FINAL TIES

A replay in the Final has been necessary on eight occasions. They have been played at:

1875	Kennington Oval	1902	Crystal Palace
1876	Kennington Oval	1910	Everton
1886	Derby	1911	Manchester (Old Trafford)
1901	Bolton	1912	Sheffield (Bramall Lane)

SUMMARY OF WINNERS

Seven times   Aston Villa

Six times   Blackburn Rovers, Newcastle United

Five times   The Wanderers

Four times   Bolton Wanderers, Sheffield United, West Bromwich Albion, Wolverhampton Wanderers and Tottenham Hotspur

Three times   Arsenal, Manchester City, Sheffield Wednesday, Manchester United.

Twice   Bury, Everton, Old Etonians, Preston North End and Nottingham Forest

Once   Barnsley, Blackburn Olympic, Blackpool, Bradford City, Burnley, Cardiff City, Charlton Athletic, Clapham Rovers, Derby County, Huddersfield Town, Notts County, Old Carthusians, Oxford University, Portsmouth, Royal Engineers and Sunderland

An Historical Survey

Football Association formed: 1863.

F.A. Cup inaugurated: 1871–72.

Football League formed: 1888.

Original members (12) – Accrington Stanley, Aston Villa, Blackburn Rovers, Bolton Wanderers, Burnley, Derby County, Everton, Notts County, Preston North End, Stoke City, West Bromwich Albion, Wolverhampton Wanderers.

Second Division formed: 1892.

Football League then comprised:
Division 1 (16 clubs) – Accrington, Aston Villa, Blackburn, Bolton, Burnley, Derby, Everton, Newton Heath (now Manchester United), Nottingham Forest, Notts County, Preston N.E., Sheffield Wednesday, Stoke, Sunderland, West Bromwich Albion, Wolverhampton Wanderers.

Division 2 (12 clubs) – Ardwick (now Manchester City), Bootle, Burslem Port Vale, Burton Swifts, Crewe Alexandra, Darwen, Grimsby Town, Lincoln City, Northwich Victoria, Sheffield United, Small Heath (now Birmingham City), Walsall Town Swifts.

Third Division South formed: 1920.
Original members (22 clubs) – Brentford, Brighton, Bristol Rovers, Crystal Palace, Exeter, Gillingham, Grimsby, Luton, Merthyr, Millwall, Newport, Northampton, Norwich, Plymouth, Portsmouth, Q.P.R., Reading, Southampton, Southend, Swansea, Swindon, Watford.

Third Division North formed: 1921.
Original members (20 clubs) – Accrington, Ashington, Barrow, Chesterfield, Crewe Alexandra, Darlington, Durham City, Grimsby Town, Halifax Town, Hartlepools United, Lincoln City, Nelson, Rochdale, Southport, Stalybridge Celtic, Stockport County, Tranmere Rovers, Walsall, Wigan Borough, Wrexham.

Third Division formed: 1958.
Original members (24 clubs) – Accrington, Bournemouth, Bradford City, Brentford, Bury, Chesterfield, Colchester, Doncaster, Halifax, Hull, Mansfield, Newport, Norwich, Notts County, Plymouth, Q.P.R., Reading, Rochdale, Southampton, Southend, Stockport, Swindon, Tranmere, Wrexham.

Fourth Division formed: 1958.

Original members (24 clubs) – Aldershot, Barrow, Bradford, Carlisle, Chester, Coventry, Crewe, Crystal Palace, Darlington, Exeter, Gateshead, Gillingham, Hartlepools, Millwall, Northampton, Oldham, Port Vale, Shrewsbury, Southport, Torquay, Walsall, Watford, Workington, York.

CHAMPIONSHIP WINS:
Arsenal seven times, Aston Villa six times, Sunderland six times.

CONSECUTIVE WINS
Huddersfield three (1923–24, 1924–25, 1925–26); Arsenal three (1932–33, 1933–34, 1934–35).

LONGEST LEAGUE RUN WITHOUT DEFEAT
Burnley, 30 games in 1920–21.

MOST POINTS
Division 1 – 1930–31: Arsenal, 66. 1960–61: Tottenham, 66.
Division 2 – 1919–20: Tottenham, 70.
Division 3 – 1960–61: Bury, 68.
Division 4 – 1960–61: Peterborough, 66.
Division 3 South – 1950–51: Nottingham Forest, 70.
                      1954–55: Bristol City, 70.
Division 3 North – 1946–47: Doncaster, 72.

LOWEST POINTS AGGREGATE
Division 1 – 1889–1890: Stoke, 10.
Division 2 – 1904–05: Doncaster, 8.
Division 3 – 1961–62: Newport, 22.
Division 4 – 1958–59: Southport, 26. 1961–62: Chester, 26.
Division 3 South – 1925–26: Q.P.R., 21. 1929–30: Merthyr, 21.
Division 3 North – 1931–32: Rochdale, 11.

MOST GOALS FOR
Division 1 – 1930–31: Aston Villa, 128.
Division 2 – 1926–27: Middlesbrough, 122.
Division 3 – 1961–62: Q.P.R., 111.
Division 4 – 1960–61: Peterborough, 134.
Division 3 South – 1927–28: Millwall, 127.
Division 3 North – 1928–29: Bradford City, 128.

MOST GOALS AGAINST
Division 1 – 1930–31: Blackpool, 125.
Division 2 – 1898–99: Darwen, 141.
Division 3 – 1959–60: Accrington S., 123.
Division 4 – 1959–60: Hartlepools U., 109.
Division 3 South – 1929–30: Merthyr, 135.
Division 3 North – 1927–28: Nelson, 136.

League Champions and F.A. Cup Winners

England – Preston (1): 1888–89.
           Aston Villa (1): 1896–97.
           Tottenham (1): 1960–61.
Scotland – Glasgow Rangers (7): 1927–28, 1929–30, 1933–34,
           1934–35, 1948–49, 1949–50, 1952–53.
           Glasgow Celtic (4): 1906–07, 1907–08, 1913–14, 1953–54.

Record Score

League: Stockport 13, Halifax 0 (6th Jan., 1934).
        Tranmere 13, Oldham 4 (26th Dec., 1935).
F.A. Cup: Preston 26, Hyde 0 (15th Oct., 1887).
Scottish Cup: Arbroath 36, Bon Accord 0 (Sept., 1885).

Highest Score

Football League: Div. 1: Aston Villa 12, Accrington 2 (1892).
                   W.B.A. 12, Darwen 0 (1892).
                   Nottingham Forest 12, Leicester 0 (1909).
           Div. 2: Newcastle 13, Newport 0 (1946).
           Div. 3: Tranmere 9, Accrington 0 (1958–59).
           Div. 4: Hartlepools 10, Barrow 1 (1958–59).
                   Wrexham 10, Hartlepools 1 (1961–62).
                   Oldham 11, Southport 0 (1962–63).
           Div. 3 South: Luton 12, Bristol Rovers 0 (1936).
           Div. 3 North: Stockport 13, Halifax 0 (1934).
                       Tranmere 13, Oldham 4 (1935).

Scottish League: Div. 1: Celtic 11, Dundee 0 (1895).
                  Airdrie 11, Falkirk 1 (1951).
                  Airdrie, 1, Hibernian 11 (1959).
           Div. 2: East Fife 13, Edinburgh City 2 (1937).

Individual League Goalscorers

Division 1 – 1927–28: Dean (Everton) 60.
Division 2 – 1926–27: Camsell (Middlesbrough) 59.
Division 3 – 1959–60: Reeves (Southampton) 39.
Division 4 – 1960–61: Bly (Peterborough) 52.
Division 3 South – 1936–37: Payne (Luton) 55.
Division 3 North: 1936–37: Harston (Mansfield) 55.
Scottish League Division 1 – 1900–01: McFadyen (Motherwell) 52.
                   Division 2 – 1927–28: Smith (Ayr) 66.

Aggregate League Goal Record

1962–63: A. Rowley (Shrewsbury) 427.

Highest Individual Goalscorers in a Match

Division 1: 7 – Ross (for Preston v. Stoke, 6th Oct., 1888).
           7 – Drake (for Arsenal v. Aston Villa, 14th Dec., 1935).
Division 2: 7 – Briggs (for Blackburn v. Bristol R., 5th Feb., 1955).
           7 – Coleman (for Stoke C. v. Lincoln, 23rd Feb., 1957).

Div. 3 South: 10 – Payne (for Luton v. Bristol R., 13th April, 1936).
Div. 3 North: 9 – Bell (for Tranmere v. Oldham, 26th Dec., 1935).

QUICK SCORING RECORD
Keetley (Lincoln v. Halifax, Div. 3 North, 1932): 5 in 20 minutes.

HIGHEST F.A. CUP FINAL WIN
1902–03: Bury 6, Derby 0.

F.A. CUP WINNERS WITHOUT CONCEDING A GOAL
Preston North End (1888–89).
Bury (1902–03).

LEAGUE CHAMPIONS WITH MAXIMUM POINTS
Glasgow Rangers (36) (1898–99).

LEAGUE CHAMPIONS WITHOUT LOSING A MATCH
Preston North End (1888–89).

HIGHEST SCORE IN INTERNATIONAL
Ireland 0, England 13 (Belfast, 1882).
England 13, Ireland 2 (Sunderland, 1899).

MOST INTERNATIONAL APPEARANCES
Billy Wright (Wolverhampton), 105 games.

RECORD ATTENDANCES
League – London: 82,905, Chelsea v. Arsenal (Stamford Bridge, 12th Oct., 1935).

Provinces: 82,950, Manchester United v. Arsenal (Maine Road, 17th Jan., 1948).

F.A. Cup – London: 126,047, Bolton v. West Ham (Wembley, 1923).

Provinces: 84,569, Manchester City v. Stoke (Maine Road, 3rd March, 1934).

Scotland: 149,547, Scotland v. England (International, Hampden Park, 17th April, 1937).

143,570, Rangers v. Hibernian (Scottish Cup, Hampden Park, 27th March, 1948).